ENGLISH 1 WORKBOOK

English as a Second Language (ESL) Level 1
Workbook for Teachers and Students
2nd Edition

TESOLCREATIONS

English 1 Workbook
English as a Second Language (ESL) Level 1
Workbook for Teachers and Students
2nd Edition

Printed in the United States of America
ISBN 979-8-218-79577-1

www.tesolcreations.com

Greetings,

This English Level 1 workbook is a collection of worksheets designed for teachers and adult students. It can be used for in-person or online classes covering vocabulary, grammar, listening, speaking, reading, and writing. Each lesson includes audio and video resources, which can be accessed by scanning the QR code on the previous page. May this workbook inspire teachers to modify the worksheets to meet the specific needs of their students.

TESOLCREATIONS

TABLE OF CONTENTS

Unit 2 – Beyond Basics

Listening and Speaking

Reading and Writing

READING

WRITING

English Grammar

Role-Play and Conversations Q and A

Role-Play

Conversations Q and A

Hello!

I am <u>Geraldine</u>.

I am _____.

name

I am from the <u>Philippines</u>.

I am from_____.

country

I am <u>40</u> years old.

I am_____years old.

age

I am a <u>teacher</u>.

I am a_____.

work

I am <u>happy</u>.

I am_____.

feeling

How about you?

It's nice to meet you!

It's nice to meet you, too!

What is your name?

I am Geraldine Woods

HELLO MY NAME IS

Where are you from?

I am from the Philippines.

Where do you live?

I live in Seattle.

Profile

Name: _____.

Student ID number: _____.

Phone number: _____.

Birthday: _____.

Complete address: _____

_____

School Email address: _____.

Personal Email address: _____.

Country: _____.

First language: _____.

Writing Practice
Hello, my name is...

My phone number is...

I live at...

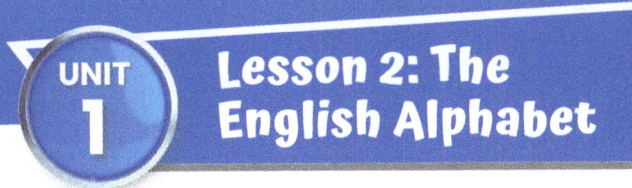

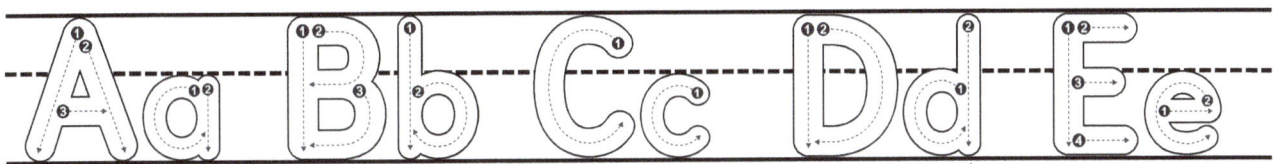

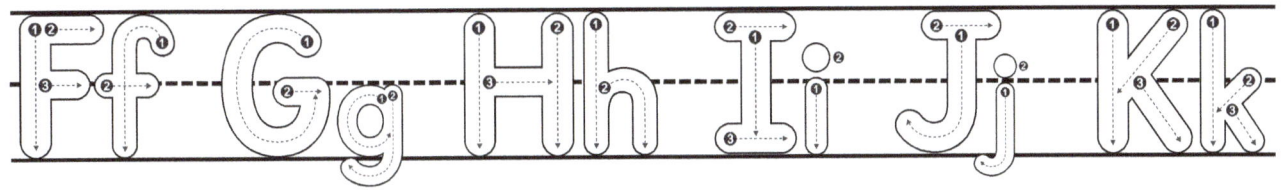

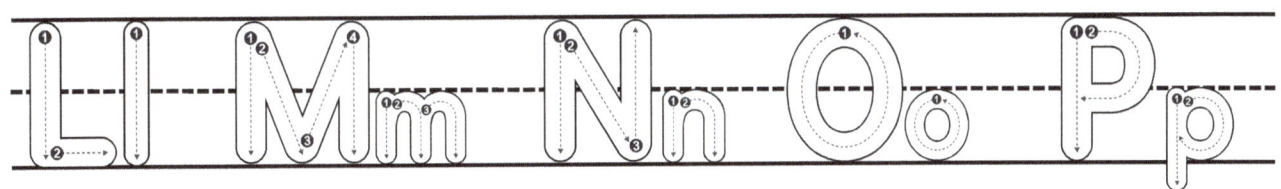

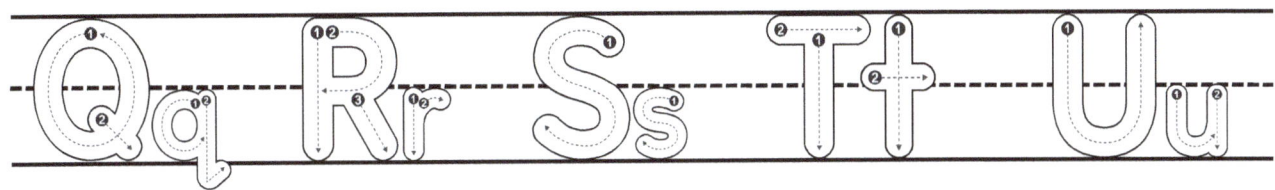

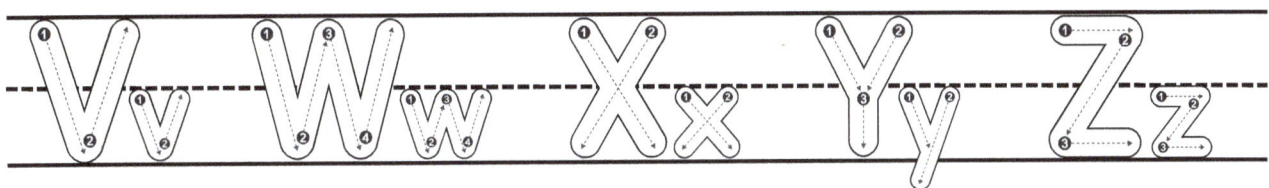

Hello

Good morning

Good afternoon

Good evening

Good night

Have a good day

See you

Take care

Goodbye

Hello

Good morning

Good afternoon

Good evening

Good night

Have a good day

See you

Take care

Goodbye

Today's English Expressions

Student A: How are you feeling today?
Student B: I feel <u>happy</u>.

I feel happy.

I feel sad.

I feel angry.

I feel sleepy.

I feel shy.

I feel tired.

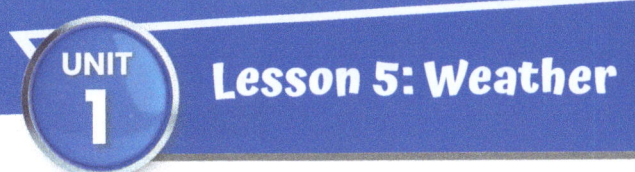

Today's English Expressions

Student A: How's the weather today?

Student B: It's <u>sunny</u>.

It's sunny.

It's cloudy.

It's rainy.

It's windy.

It's stormy.

It's snowy.

It's foggy.

It's hot.

It's cold.

Today's English Expressions

Student A: What day is it?

Student B: It's <u>Friday</u>.

Sunday

Monday

Tuesday

Wednesday

Thursday

Friday

Saturday

Days

PRACTICE

Sun

Mon

Tue

Wed

Thu

Fri

Sat

Today's English Expressions

Student A: When is Valentine's day?

Student B: It's <u>in February</u>.

It's <u>on February 14</u>.

January
February 
March 
April 
May 
June 
July 
August 
September 
October 
November 
December

UNIT 1

Lesson 8: Seasons and Temperature

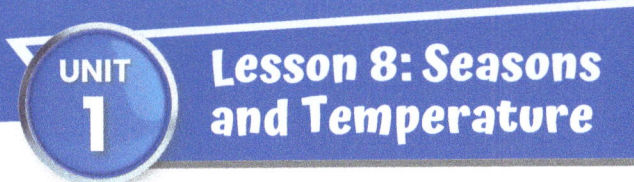

Today's English Expressions

It's spring. It's warm.

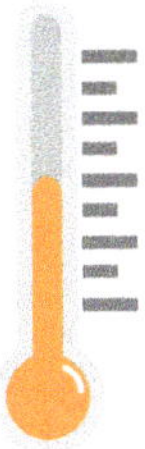

Spring - It's warm.

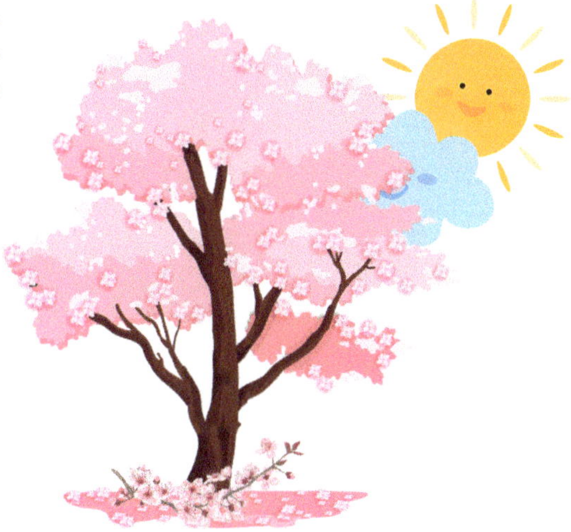

Summer - It's hot.

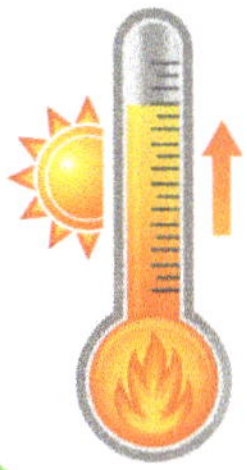

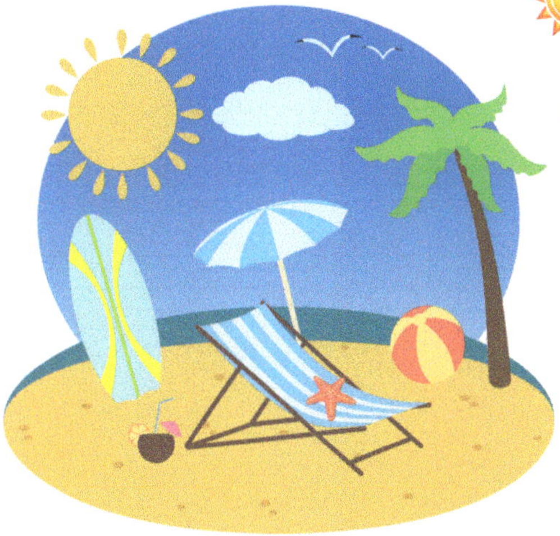

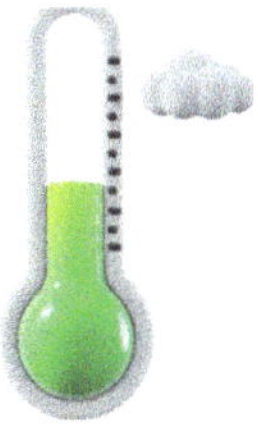

Fall- It's cool.

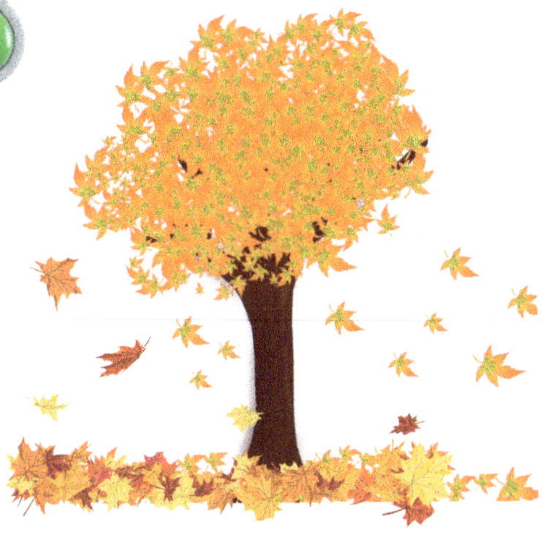

Winter - It's cold.

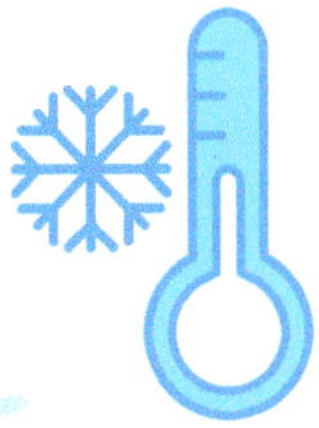

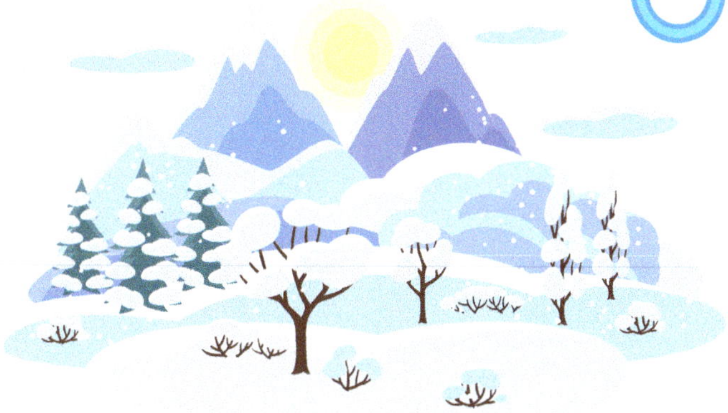

UNIT 1

Lesson 9: Colors

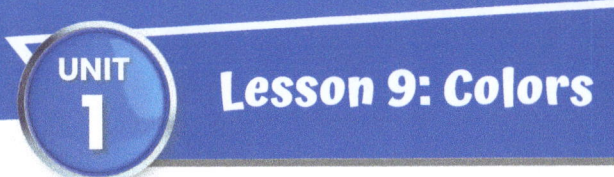

Today's English Expressions

Student A: Do you like red?

Student B: Yes, I do. / No, I don't.

white

red

orange

yellow

green

blue

purple

violet

brown

black

pink

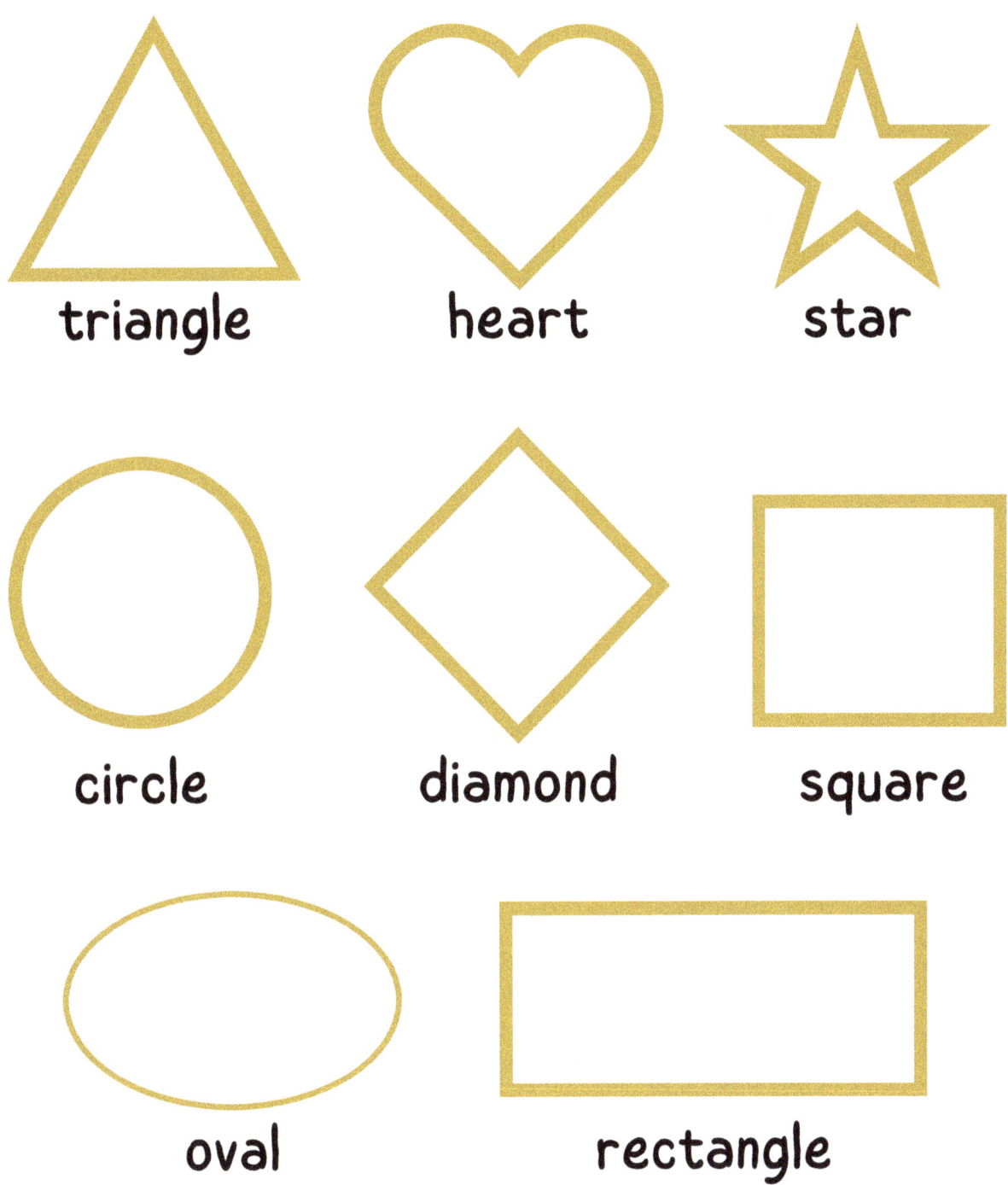

triangle   heart   star

circle   diamond   square

oval   rectangle

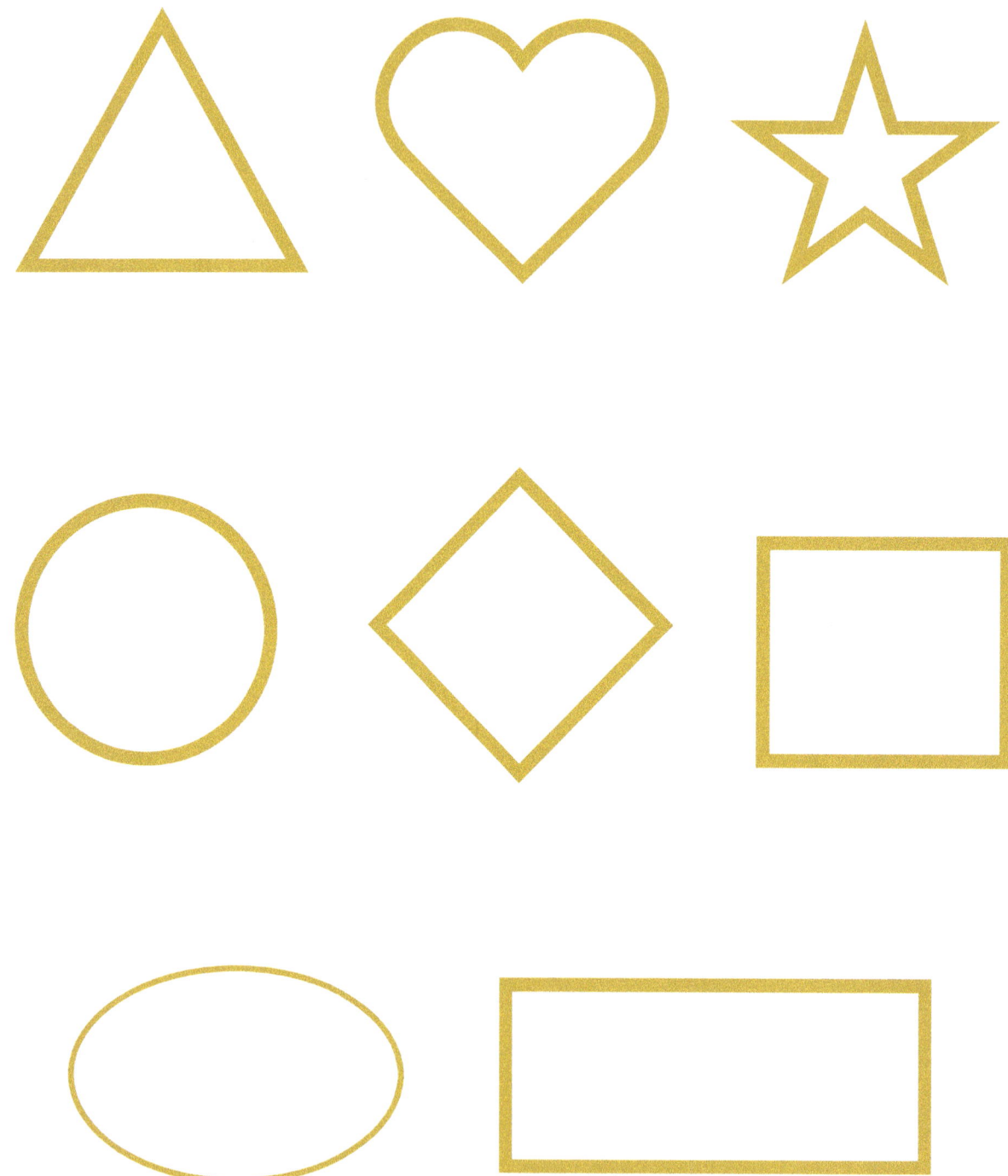

Today's English Expressions

Student A: What is the date today?

Student B: Today is <u>Monday, December 25th</u>.

Today is <u>Monday, December 25, 2023</u>.

calendar

weekday

weekend ⏜ ⏜ **weekend**

Sun	Mon	Tue	Wed	Thu	Fri	Sat
					1 first	**2** second
3 third	**4** fourth	**5** fifth	**6** sixth	**7** seventh	**8** eighth	**9** ninth
10 tenth	**11** eleventh	**12** twelfth	**13** thirteenth	**14** fourteenth	**15** fifteenth	**16** sixteenth
17 seventeenth	**18** eighteenth	**19** nineteenth	**20** twentieth	**21** twenty-first	**22** twenty-second	**23** twenty-third
24 twenty-fourth	**25** twenty-fifth	**26** twenty-sixth	**27** twenty-seventh	**28** twenty-eighth	**29** twenty-ninth	**30** thirtieth
31 thirty-first						

December — **week**

Ordinal Numbers

1st first	11th eleventh	21st twenty-first	31st thirty-first
2nd second	12th twelfth	22nd twenty-second	
3rd third	13th thirteenth	23rd twenty-third	
4th fourth	14th fourteenth	24th twenty-fourth	
5th fifth	15th fifteenth	25th twenty-fifth	
6th sixth	16th sixteenth	26th twenty-sixth	
7th seventh	17th seventeenth	27th twenty-seventh	
8th eighth	18th eighteenth	28th twenty-eighth	
9th ninth	19th nineteenth	29th twenty-ninth	
10th tenth	20th twentieth	30th thirtieth	

zero	ten	twenty	thirty
one	eleven	twenty-one	forty
two	twelve	twenty-two	fifty
three	thirteen	twenty-three	sixty
four	fourteen	twenty -four	seventy
five	fifteen	twenty-five	eighty
six	sixteen	twenty-six	ninety
seven	seventeen	twenty-seven	one hundred
eight	eighteen	twenty-eight	one thousand
nine	nineteen	twenty-nine	one million

Cardinal Numbers

0	10	20	30
1	11	21	40
2	12	22	50
3	13	23	60
4	14	24	70
5	15	25	80
6	16	26	90
7	17	27	100
8	18	28	1000
9	19	29	1,000,000

UNIT 1 — Lesson 13: Time

Today's English Expressions

Student A: What time is it?

Student B: It is <u>six o'clock</u>.

It's <u>six o'clock</u>.

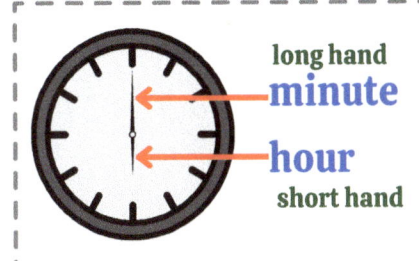

long hand
minute
hour
short hand

 It's twelve o'clock.
It's noon.

 It's six o'clock.

 It's one o'clock.

 It's seven o'clock.

 It's two o'clock.

 It's eight o'clock.

 It's three o'clock.

 It's nine o'clock.

 It's four o'clock.

 It's ten o'clock.

 It's five o'clock.

 It's eleven o'clock.

It's 1:05.

It's 1:35.

It's 1:10.

It's 1:40.

It's 1:15.

It's 1:45.

It's 1:20.

It's 1:50.

It's 1:25.

It's 1:55.

It's 1:30.

It's 2:00.

Lesson 14: Classroom English

 Please stand.

 Please sit.

 Please write.

 Please read.

 Please look.

 Please listen.

 Please talk.

 Please circle the LETTER.

 Please raise your hand.

 Please close your book.

 Please open your book.

 Please say, "Hello."

 Please repeat, "Hi!"

 Please pair up.

 Please make groups.

 Please turn to page 8.

Good morning!    Good morning!

It's nice to meet you!   It's nice to meet you too!

How are you?   I am fine, thank you.
                      I'm fine, thank you.

Good afternoon!   Good afternoon!

Good evening!   Good evening!

What is <u>your</u> name?   <u>I</u> am Geraldine.
                       I'm Geraldine.

Please spell your name.   It is G E R A L D I N E.
                       It's G E R A L D I N E.

How's the weather today?   It is rainy.
                       It's rainy.

What day is it?   It is Monday.
                  It's Monday.

What is the date today?   It is January 11, 2023.
                       It's January 11, 2023.

What time is it?   It is nine o'clock.
                  It's nine o'clock.

Have a good day!   You too!

See you!   See you!

Goodbye!   Goodbye!

Good morning!

Good morning!

It's nice to meet you!

It's nice to meet you too!

How are you?

I am fine, thank you.
I'm fine, thank you.

Good afternoon!

Good afternoon!

Good evening!

Good evening!

What is your name?

I am Geraldine.
I'm Geraldine.

Please spell your name.

It is G E R A L D I N E
It's G E R A L D I N E

How's the weather today?

It is rainy.
It's rainy.

What day is it?

It is Monday.
It's Monday.

What is the date today?

It is January 11, 2023.
It's January 11, 2023.

What time is it?

It is nine o'clock.
It's nine o'clock.

Have a good day!

You too!

See you!

See you!

Goodbye!

Goodbye!

What is your full name?

My name is Geraldine Elle Woods.

What is your first name?

My first name is Geraldine.

What is your middle name?

My middle name is Elle.

What is your last name?

My last name is Woods.

When is your birthday?

My birthday is **in December**.
My birthday is **on December 25th**.
My birthday is **on December 25, 1983**.

Unit Test: Match pictures and lessons.

Alphabet / Cardinal Numbers / Classroom
English / Color / Day/ Date / Feelings /
Greetings / Ordinal Numbers / Month /
Shape / Seasons / Time / Weather

Greetings

UNIT 2

Lesson 16: Personal Information

Complete Name	Geraldine Elle Woods
Address	12345 10th Avenue NW, Apt. M-11 Seattle, WA 98100.
Phone Number	253-123-4567
Birthdate (mm-dd-yyyy)	12-25-1983
Country	Philippines
First Language	Cebuano
Email address	Geraldine.Woods@gmail.com
Height	4 feet 11 inches / 4' 11"
Weight	80 pounds (lbs.) / 36 kilograms (kgs.)
Eye color	brown (BRN)
Hair color	black (BLK)

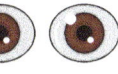

Personal Information

Complete Name	
Address	
Phone Number	
Birthdate (mm-dd-yyyy)	
Country	
First Language	
Email address	
Height	
Weight	
Eye Color	
Hair Color	

A. Read the information in the ID. Answer the questions.

WA USA **WASHINGTON**

DRIVER'S LICENSE
FEDERAL LIMITS APPLY

4D LIC# ABC12345678A   9 CLASS
1 WOODS
2 GERALDINE ELLE   4a ISS 04/03/2023
3 DOB 12/25/1983
8 12345 10th Avenue NW
   Seattle, WA 98100
15 SEX F   18 EYES BRO
16 HGT 4'-11"   17 WGT 90 lb
12 RESTRICTIONS   9a END NONE
         NONE   4b EXP 03/23/2029
DD5 ABC 12345678ABO403230123567

Geraldine Woods

1. What is her first name? _____
2. What is her middle name? _____
3. What is her last name? _____
4. When is her birthday? _____
5. Where is her address? _____
6. How tall is she? _____

B. Read the information in the ID. Complete the sentences.

South Seattle College

Student ID
Geraldine E. Woods
ID: 0617111822

1. Her first name is _____ .

2. Her middle initial is _____ .

3. Her last name is _____ .

4. Her student ID number is _____ .

5. Geraldine is a student at _____ .

Speaking Test
Who? What? Where? When? Why? How?

Let's practice!

1. What is your full name (complete name)? My full name is Geraldine Elle Woods.

2. What is your first name? My first name is Geraldine.

3. What is your middle name? My middle name is Elle. OR (I do not have a middle name.)

4. What is your last name? My last name is Woods.

5. Where are you from? I am from the Philippines.

6. In which city did you live in your country? I lived in Cebu City, Philippines.

7. Where do you live now? I live in Seattle.

8. How long have you been in the US? I have been in the US for three years now.

9. What is your first language? My first language is Cebuano.

10. What do you do? I am a student. OR (I am a homemaker.)

11. When is your birthday? My birthday is on December 25, 1983.

12. How old are you? I'm 40 years old.

13. How many family members do you have? My family has 5 members: my husband, Rob, three children, and me. My children are Devine, 18 years old, Nicole, 16 years old, and Junior, 5 months old.

14. What is your hobby? My hobby is watching movies.

15. What is your favorite food in your country? My favorite food in my country is Chicken Lumpia.

16. What is your favorite place in your country? My favorite place in my country is Cebu City.

17. What is your complete address? It's 12345 10th Avenue NW, Apt. M-11 Seattle, WA. 98100.

18. What is your street number? It's 12345 10th Avenue NW.

19. What is your apartment number? It's apartment M-11.

20. What's your ZIP code? It's 98100.

21. What is your phone number? It's 253-123-4567.

22. What is your email address? It's geraldine.woods@seattleschool.edu.

Answer the questions.

1. What is your full name (complete name)?

2. What is your first name?

3. What is your middle name?

4. What is your last name?

5. Where are you from?

6. In which city did you live in your country?

7. Where do you live now?

8. How long have you been in the US?

9. What is your first language?

10. What do you do?

11. When is your birthday?

12. How old are you?

13. How many family members do you have?

14. What is your hobby?

15. What is your favorite food in your country?

16. What is your favorite place in your country?

17. What is your complete address?

18. What is your street number?

19. What is your apartment number?

20. What's your ZIP code?

21. What is your phone number?

22. What is your email address?

Today's English Expressions

I wake up at 4 am.
I go to bed at 9 pm.

 wake up

 make my bed

 take a bath

 brush my teeth

 comb my hair

 get dressed

 eat breakfast

 drive to school

 take a bus

 walk to school

 study English

 eat lunch

 go to work

 start my work

 shop with a friend

 play with my friends

 go home

 clean my house

 vacuum the floor

 take care of my child

 wash dishes

 do the laundry

 fold clothes

 exercise

 cook dinner

 eat dinner

 do my homework

 surf the net

 watch TV

 pray

 go to bed

Daily Routine

ENGLISH PHRASES - Daily Routine

Past Tense	Present Tense
cooked	cook
took care of my child	take care of my child
cleaned the house	clean the house
did laundry	do laundry
walked to the park	walk to the park
exercised	exercise
read a book	read a book
watched a movie	watch a movie
listened to music	listen to music
slept	sleep
went shopping	go shopping
went to a meeting	go to a meeting
went to work	go to work
worked all day	work all day

Today's English Expressions

This is Rob. He is my husband.

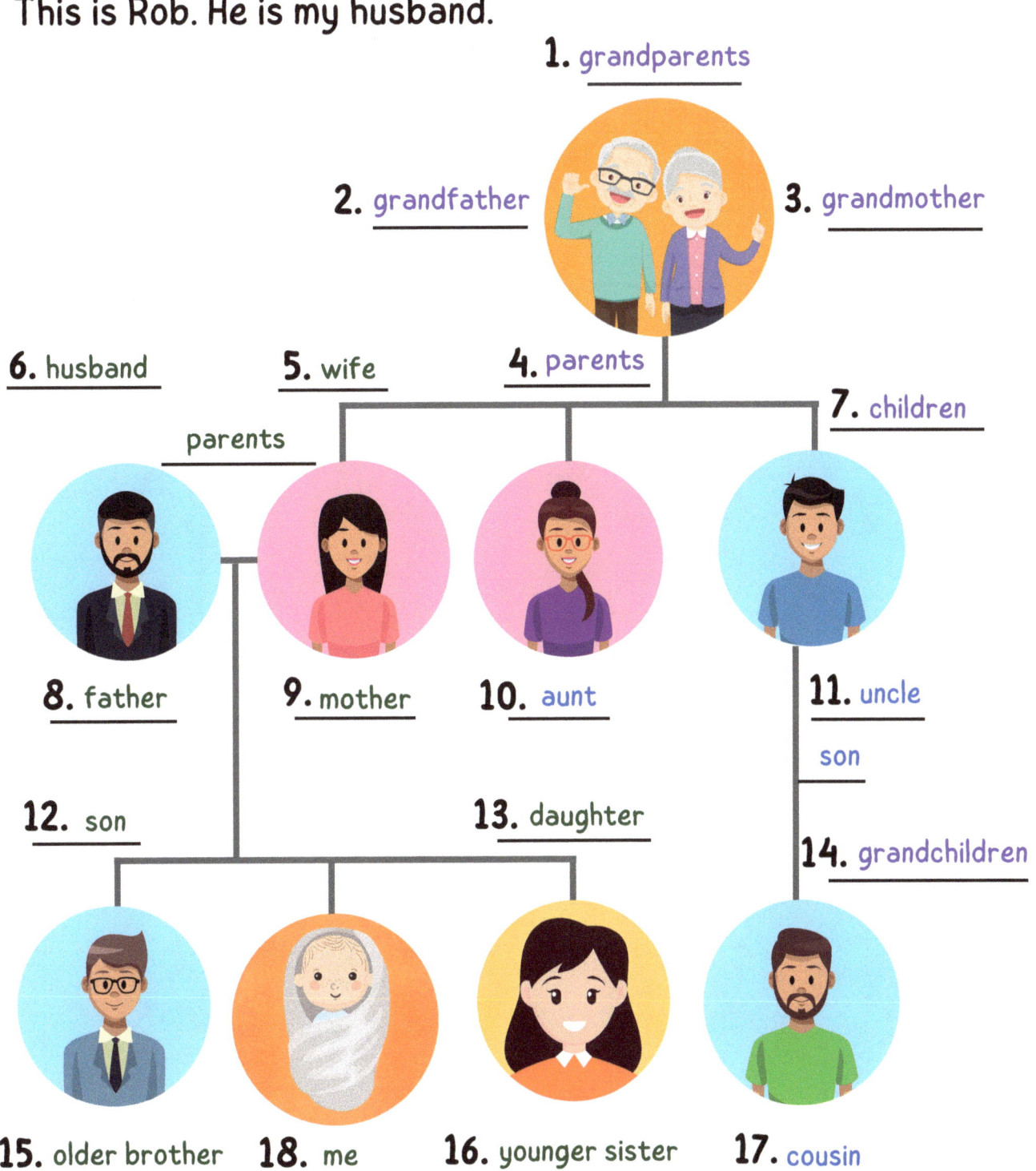

1. grandparents

2. grandfather

3. grandmother

6. husband

5. wife

4. parents

7. children

parents

8. father

9. mother

10. aunt

11. uncle

son

12. son

13. daughter

14. grandchildren

15. older brother

18. me

16. younger sister

17. cousin

My Family Tree

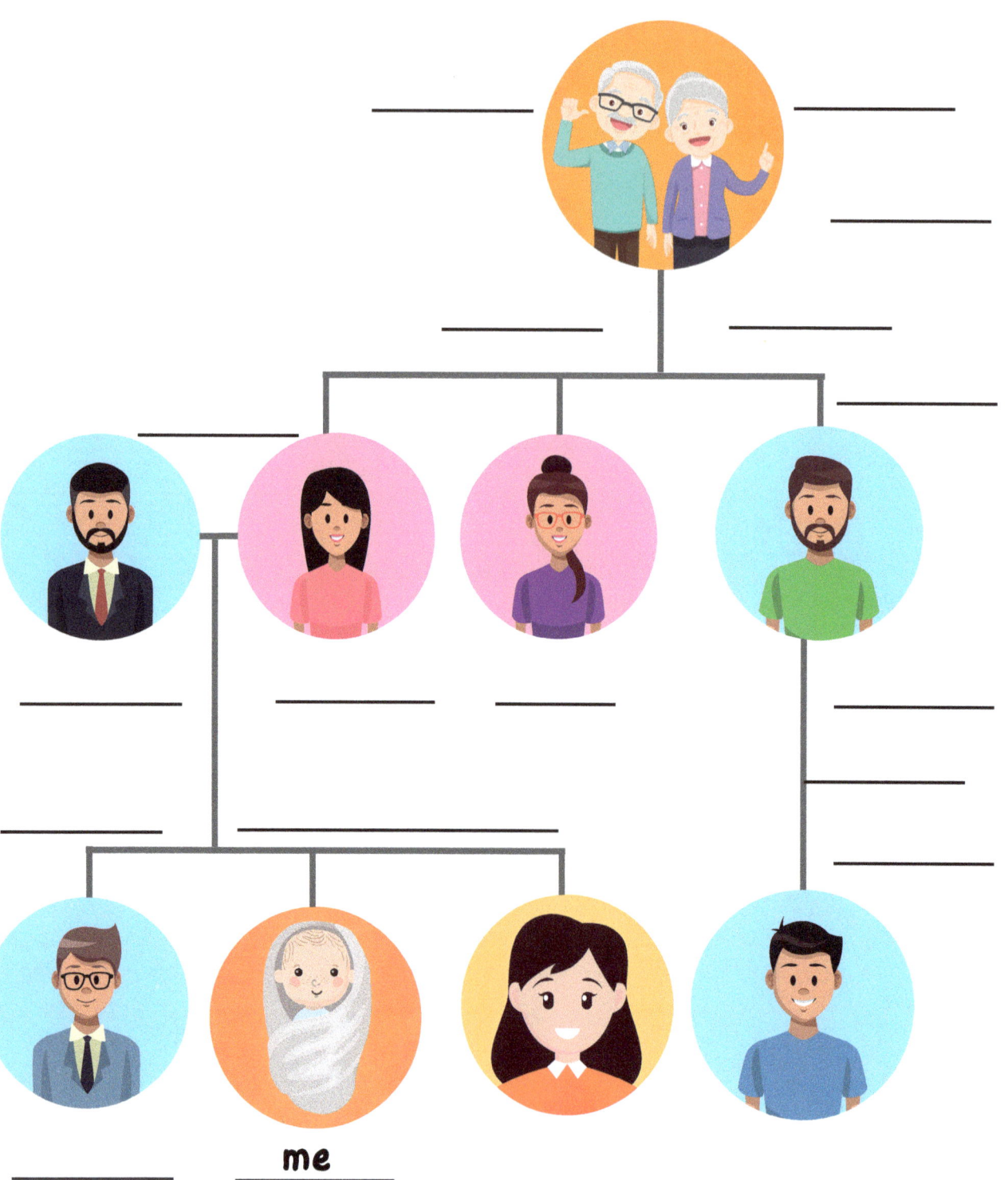

me

ENGLISH PHRASES - FAMILY

have dinner together

play games.

watch movies.

go for a picnic.

take family photos.

go on a trip.

have a family gathering

help with homework

celebrate birthdays.

read bedtime stories .

How many family members do you have?

There are five: my husband, Rob, three children, and me. My children are Devine, 18 years old, Nicole, 16 years old, and Junior, 5 months old.

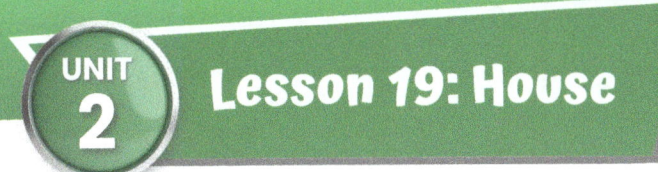

Today's English Expressions

My home has <u>two bedrooms, a living room, a dining room, a kitchen, a bathroom, and a garage</u>.

bathroom

bedroom

dining room

garage

kitchen

living room

Yard Sale

Circle the items you see at the yard sale.

bed	bookcase	cabinet	chairs
couch	dresser	fork	kettle
lamp	mirror	pans	plate
pots	spoon	table	toys

Things at Home

bed

bookcase

table

chairs

cabinet

couch

dresser

kettle

lamp

mirror

pan

fork

plate

spoon

glass

pot

Appliances

Check the items you see at the sale.

air conditioner   hair dryer   sewing machine

blender   heater   slow cooker

cellphone   iPad   stereo

coffee maker   iron   television

computer   laptop   toaster

dishwasher   microwave oven   vacuum cleaner

dryer   oven   water heater

electric kettle   rice cooker   washing machine

food processor   refrigerator   water purifier

sleep in the bedroom.

relax in the living room.

take a shower in the bathroom

cook meals in the kitchen.

have meals in the dining room.

wash dishes in the sink.

park your car in the garage.

head

face

hair

forehead

eyebrow

ear

eye

cheek

mouth

nose

neck

shoulder

arm

chest

hand

stomach

finger

leg

foot

knee

ankle

toe

heel

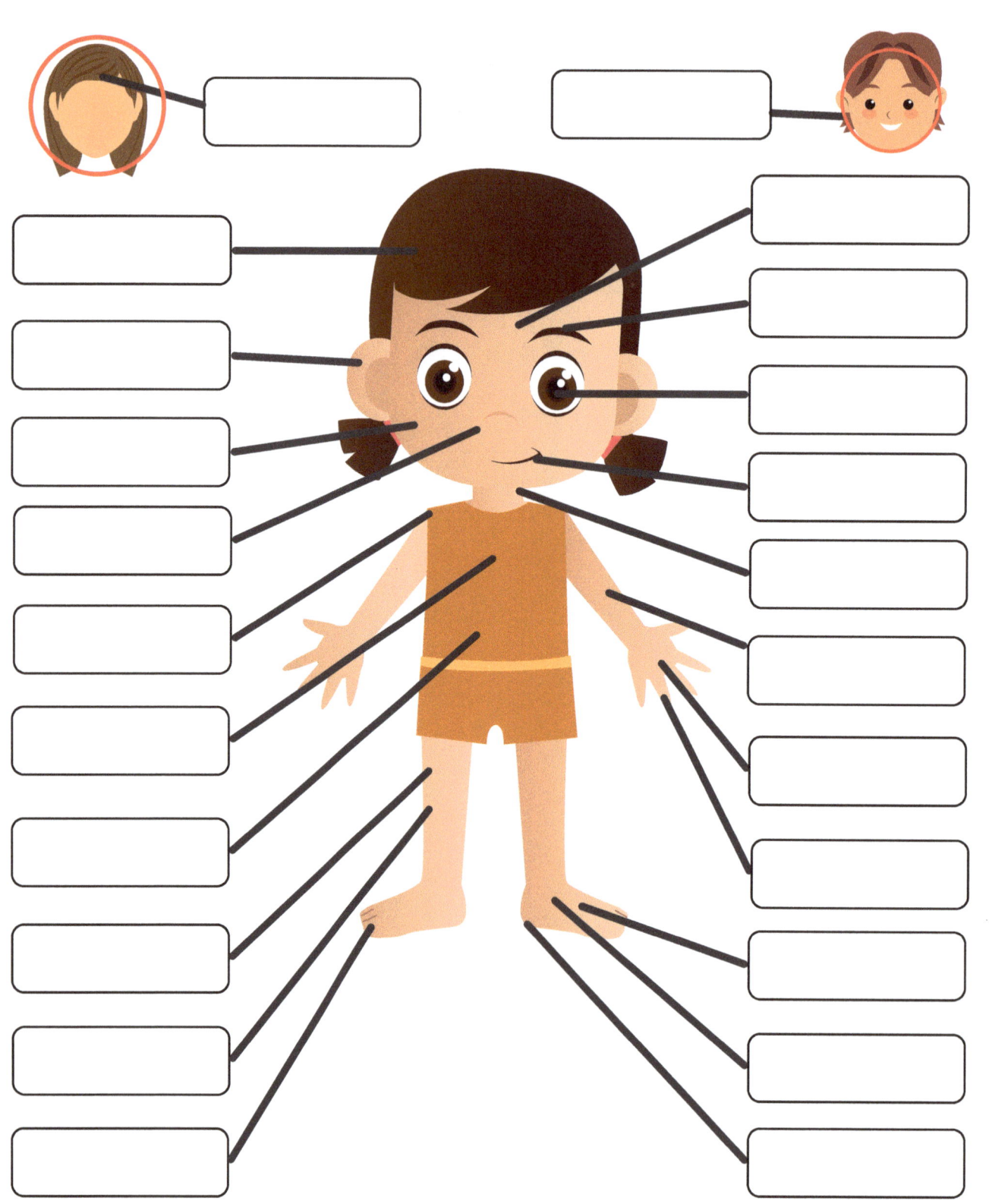

blow your nose

brush your hair

clap your hands

pat your shoulders

shake your head

snap your fingers

stomp your feet

wash your face

wave your arms

wipe your eyes

Today's English Expressions

Student A: What's the matter?

Student B: I have a <u>headache</u>.

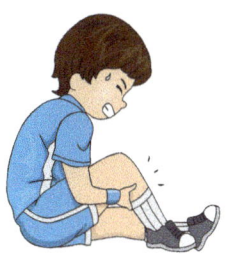

I have a
cramp.

I have
a cold.

I have
a cough.

I have an
earache.

I have a
fever.

I have a
headache.

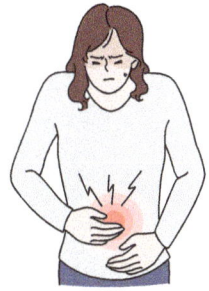

I have a
stomach ache.

I have a
sore throat.

I have a
toothache.

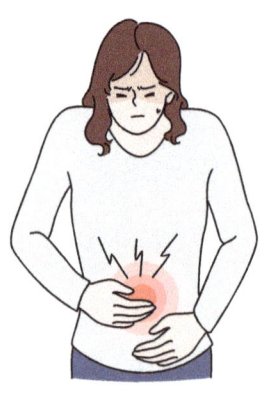  

take a break.

take your medicine.

drink lots of water.

get enough sleep.

wash your hands.

cover your mouth when you cough

eat healthy foods.

stay active and play.

avoid too much sugar.

remember to wear sunscreen

Lesson 22: School Supplies

Today's English Expressions
Student A: What is it?
Student B: It's a <u>pen</u>.

bag

book

chair

clock

computer

crayon

desk

eraser

folder

globe

glue

highlighter

laptop

marker

notebook

paper

paper clip

pen

pencil

pencil case

pencil sharpener

projector

projector screen

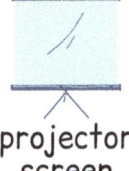
push pin

ruler

scissors

stapler

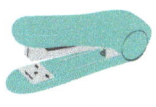
table

tape

white board

School Supplies

     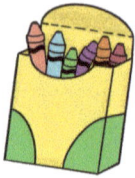

   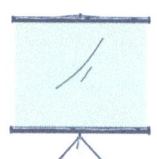  

 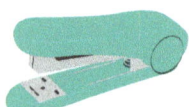   

color with crayons

cut with scissors

draw with markers

glue the paper

pack my bag

sharpen the pencil

staple the papers

tape the box

use the eraser

write with a pen

Today's English Expressions

Student A: <u>There is</u> a computer.

Student B: <u>There are</u> two computers.

computer

laptop

keyboard

mouse

Bluetooth

cable

charger

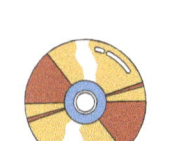

compact disc (CD)

Central Processing
Unit (CPU)

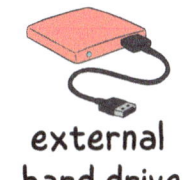

external
hard drive

Universal Serial
Bus (USB)
flash drive

headphones

Secure
Digital card(SD)
or memory card

microphone

modem

printer

router

scanner

speaker

webcam or
video camera

Wi-Fi

Computer Words

  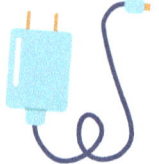 

charge the laptop

click the mouse

connect to Bluetooth

connect to Wi-Fi

insert an SD card

print out homework

type on the keyboard

use a flash drive

use headphones

use the speaker

Today's English Expressions

Student A: What do you do?

Student B: I am a <u>teacher</u>.

chef

courier

doctor

firefighter

flight attendant

nurse

pilot

photographer

police officer

postal worker

scientist

secretary

server

soldier

taxi driver

teacher

vet

arrange things in storage

count items for inventory

deliver orders

drive a forklift machine

help customers

lift and move heavy boxes

push the cart

put things on store shelves

scan items

work together with my team

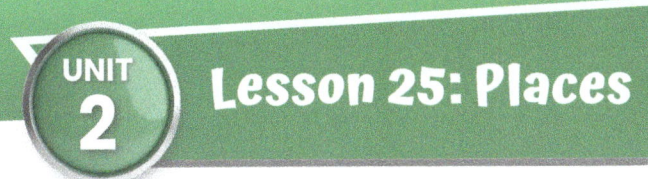

UNIT 2 — Lesson 25: Places

Today's English Expressions

Student A: Where is the grocery store?

Student B: The grocery store is <u>across from</u> the school.

bakery

bank

barbershop

cafe

church

fire station

flower shop

gas station

grocery store

hospital

house

library

mall

park

pet shop

police station

post office

restaurant

school

buy bread at the bakery

get money from the bank

get a haircut at the barbershop

buy coffee at the cafe

pray at the church

pray at the mosque

call the fire station

get help at the police station

buy flowers at the flower shop

fill up my car at the gas station

buy food at the grocery store

go home

see a doctor at the hospital

read books at the library

shop at the mall

go to the pet shop

buy food at the grocery store

send a package to the post office

eat at the restaurant

study at school

airplane

bus

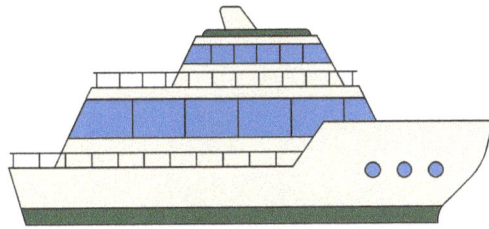

boat

bicycle

car

scooter

train

van

Transharmony

PRACTICE

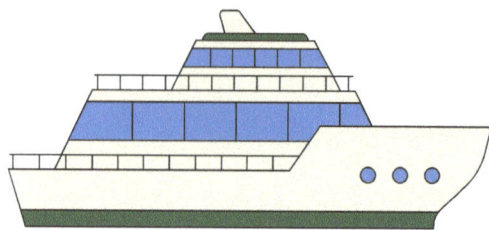

ENGLISH PHRASES - Transportation

catch the bus

drive a car

drive a van

fly on a plane

get a taxi

get off the train

hop on a train

ride a bike

sail on a ship

walk to school

Today's English Expressions

Student A: How much is the ice cream?

Student B: It's one dollar.

BILLS

COINS

quarter   dime

nickel   penny

BILLS

_____

_____   _____

_____   _____

_____   _____

COINS

_____   _____

_____   _____

pay with cash.

pay with a debit card

use a credit card.

put the card in the machine

deposit the money.

withdraw the money.

count your coins.

count your money.

Today's English Expressions

Student A: What clothes do you like to wear?

Student B: I like to wear a <u>dress</u>.

blazer

blouse

coat

dress

hoodie

shirt

suit

sweater

t-shirt

skirt

short pants

jeans

pants

scarf

gloves

belt

socks

Clothes

ask for help

check the price

check the receipt

choose a style

find your size

look for a sale

pay at the cashier

pick a color

try it on

use the mirror

Today's English Expressions

Student A: What fruit do you like?

Student B: I like <u>apples</u>.

apple

avocado

banana

berries

cherry

coconut

grapes

kiwi

lemon

mango

orange

papaya

pear

peach

pineapple

strawberry

watermelon

cut the apple

peel the apple

slice the apple

dice the mango

mash the avocado.

peel the banana

split the coconut.

squeeze the lemon.

wash the berries.

deseed a pomegrenate.

Lesson 30: Vegetables

UNIT 2

Today's English Expressions

Student A: What vegetables do you like?

Student B: I like <u>carrots and eggplants</u>.

asparagus

broccoli

Brussels sprouts

cabbage

carrot

cauliflower

celery

corn

cucumber

eggplant

garlic

ginger

green onion

mushroom

onion

potato

peas

green and red bell pepper

pumpkin

radish

spinach

tomato

103

blanch the spinach.

boil the peas

chop the celery.

cut the asparagus

dice the carrot

fry the cauliflower.

grill the corn.

shred the cabbage.

slice the cucumber.

steam the broccoli.

Today's English Expressions

Student A: What is your favorite sport?

Student B: My favorite sport is <u>football</u>.

archery

badminton

baseball

basketball

cycling

fencing

football

golf

skating

soccer

tennis

volleyball

ENGLISH PHRASES - Sports

aim at the target.

hit the shuttlecock.

throw the ball.

dribble the ball

pedal faster.

wield your sword.

kick the ball

glide smoothly

serve the ball

hit the ball into the hole

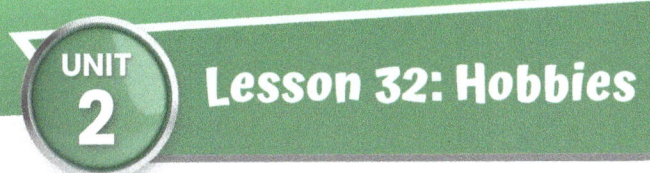

Today's English Expressions

Student A: What is your hobby?

Student B: My hobby is <u>watching movies</u>.

My hobbies are <u>cooking and watching movies</u>.

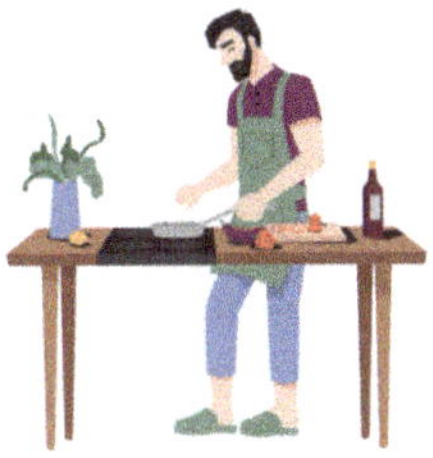

cooking

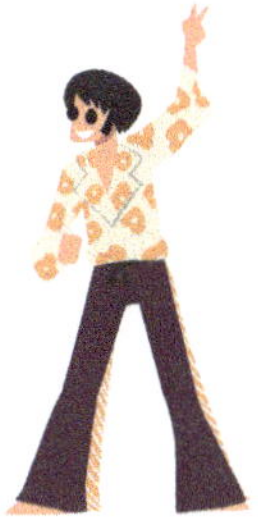

dancing

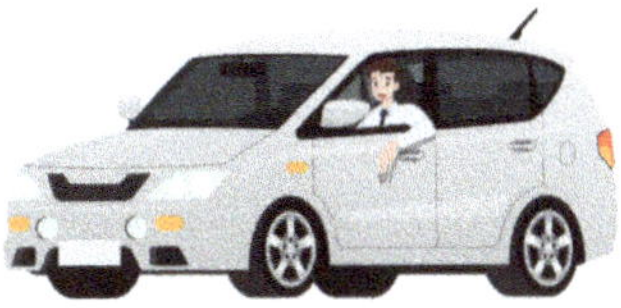

driving

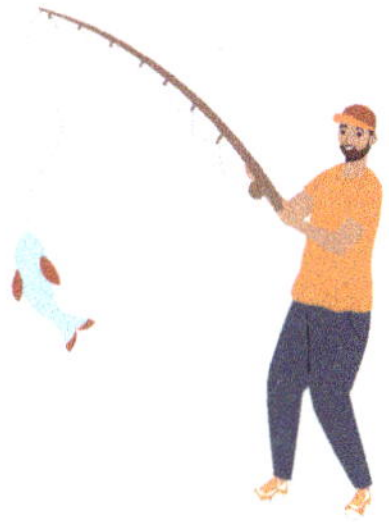

fishing

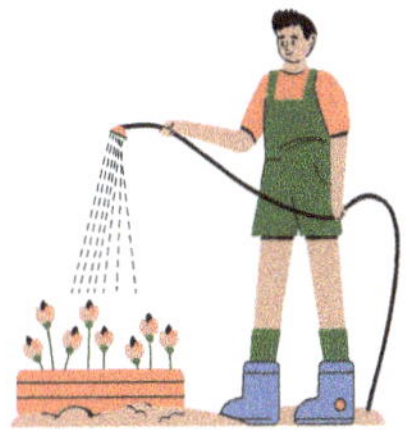

gardening

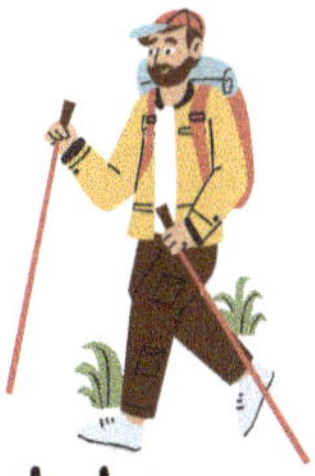

hiking

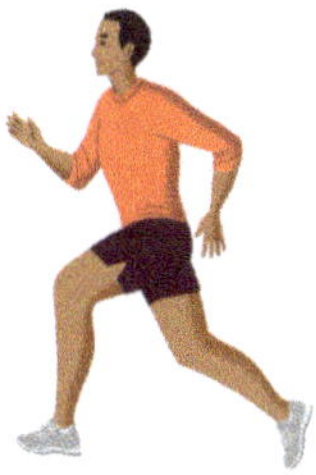

jogging

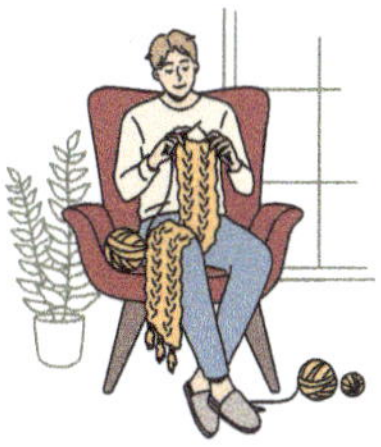

knitting

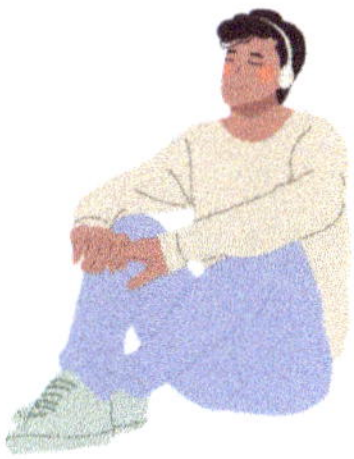

listening to music

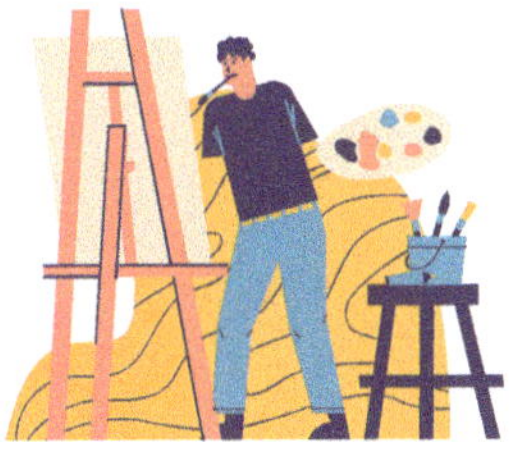

painting

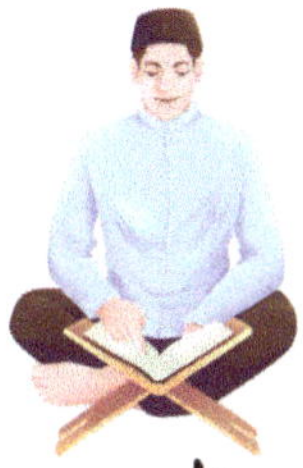

reading

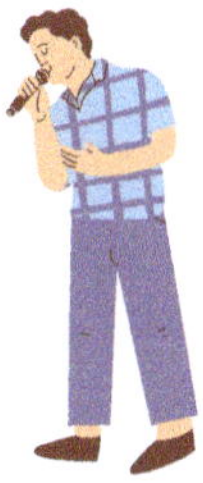

singing

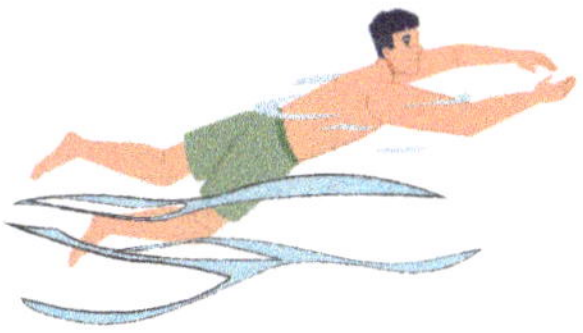

swimming

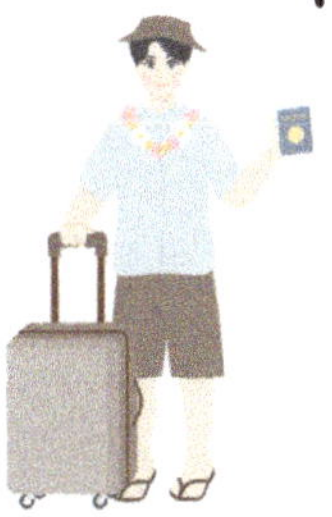

traveling

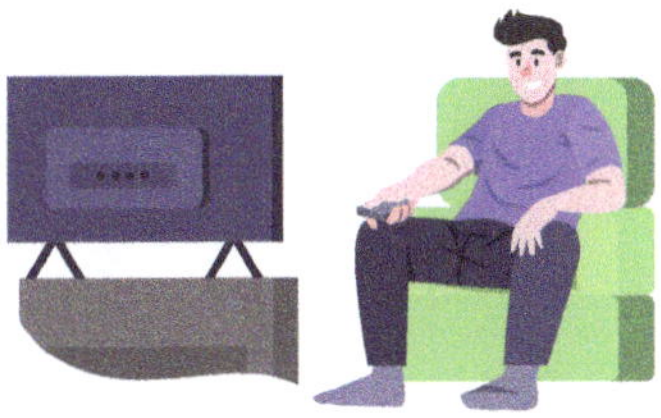

watching movies

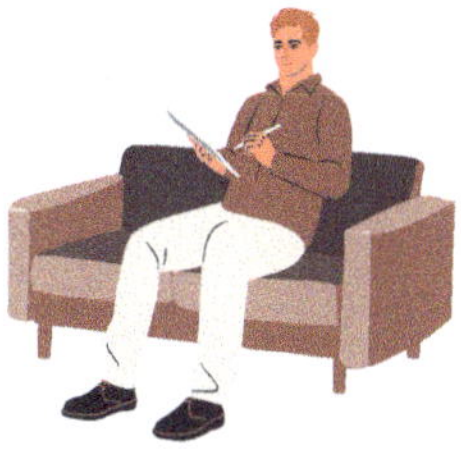

writing

Hobbies

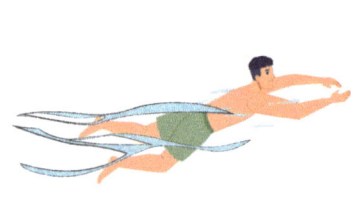   

cooking for the family

dancing at parties.

driving out of town

fishing by the lake.

gardening with mom.

hiking in nature.

jogging in the park.

knitting a scarf.

painting a picture.

reading adventure books

LISTENING AND SPEAKING

Listen. Match pictures and sentences. Write the letters A, B, C, D inside the box.

A.

B.

C.

D.

1.	2.	3.	4.

ANSWERS:
D 1. I exercise every day.
A 2. I cook dinner for my family.
B 3. I study English every night.
C 4. I like to watch videos on my laptop.

Listen and complete the paragraph.

a. bear   b. brother   c. family   d. mother   e. name   f. years

Hello! I am Ana. This is my 1. _____: my grandfather, grandmother, father, mother, older sister, and younger 2. _____ . My grandfather's 3. _____ is Carl and my grandmother's name is Esme. My father's name is Edward. He is a farmer. My 4. _____'s name is Bella. She is a homemaker. My older sister is Alice. She is 11 years old. She likes her teddy 5. _____ very much. My younger brother is Emmett. He is three 6. _____ old. I love my family.

ANSWERS: 1.c 2.b 3.e 4.d 5.a 6.f

Listen. Match pictures and sentences. Write the letters A, B, C, D inside the box.

1.	2.	3.	4.

ANSWERS:

C.1. This living room has a small window, a couch, a round table in the middle, a desk with drawers, some bookshelves, and some toys.

A.2. This living room has a big window, a couch with bookshelves behind it, a desk with drawers, a round table, a TV with plants on each side, and pictures of bugs and leaves on the wall.

D.3. This living room has a couch in front of the window. Next to the couch, you will find bookshelves and a cabinet. Across from the couch is a TV with a plant next to it. The wall has a clock and pictures of bugs. Plus, there is a coat hanger in the room.

B.4. This living room has a couch in front of the window and a plant beside it. On a table, there is a computer and another bookshelf above it. The wall has pictures of leaves, and there is also a clock on it.

Listen and answer the questions. Write the body parts inside the box.

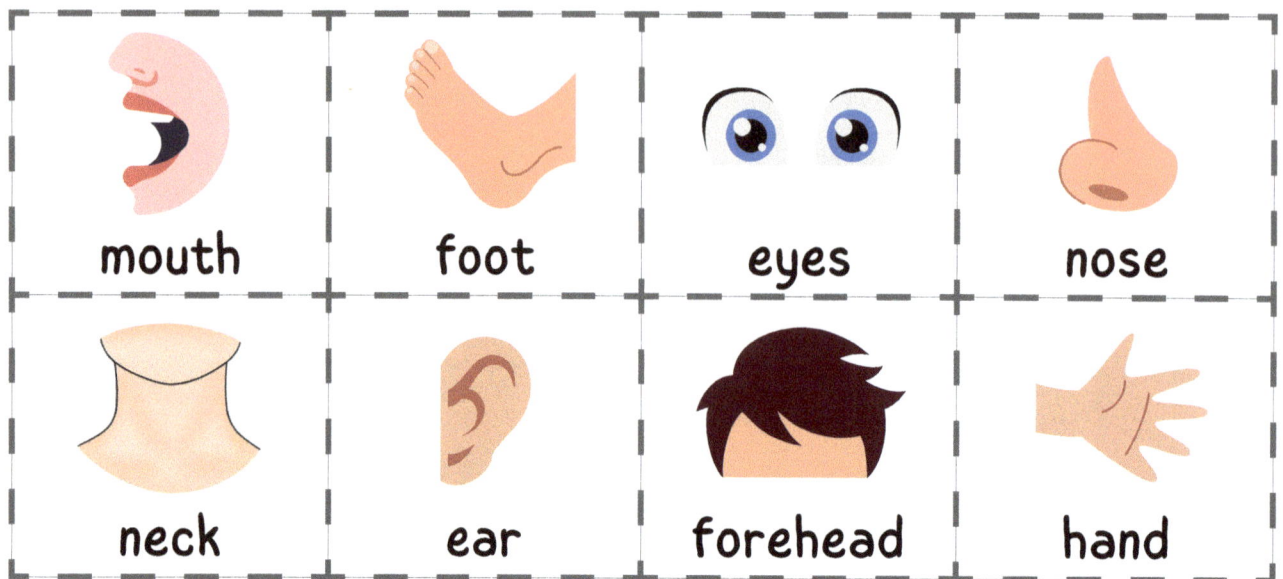

1.	2.	3.	4.
5.	6.	7.	8.

ANSWERS:
1. What do you use to see? — eyes
2. What do you use to eat? — mouth
3. What do you use to hear? — ear
4. What do you use to smell? — nose
5. How do you move your head? — neck
6. What do you use to kick a ball? — foot
7. What do you use to feel things? — hand
8. Where are your eyebrows on your face? — forehead

Listen. Match pictures and sentences. Write the letters A, B, C inside the box.

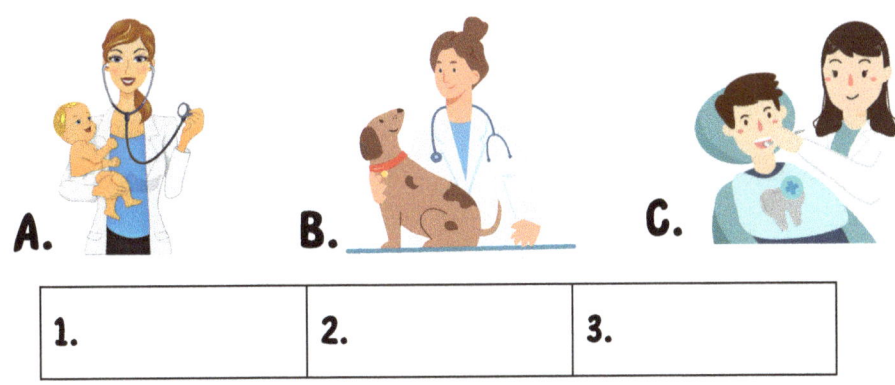

A. **B.** **C.**

1.	2.	3.

ANSWERS:

B 1. Hello! I'm a veterinarian. I help sick animals get better. I care for dogs, cats, and more to make them healthy and happy.

C 2. Hello! I'm a dentist. I help people care for their teeth and make sure their smiles stay bright and healthy.

A 3. Hello! I'm a pediatrician. I take care of babies and make them feel well. I help babies when they are sick so they can grow up strong and happy.

Listen to the conversations. Match pictures and sentences. Write the letters A, B, C, D inside the box.

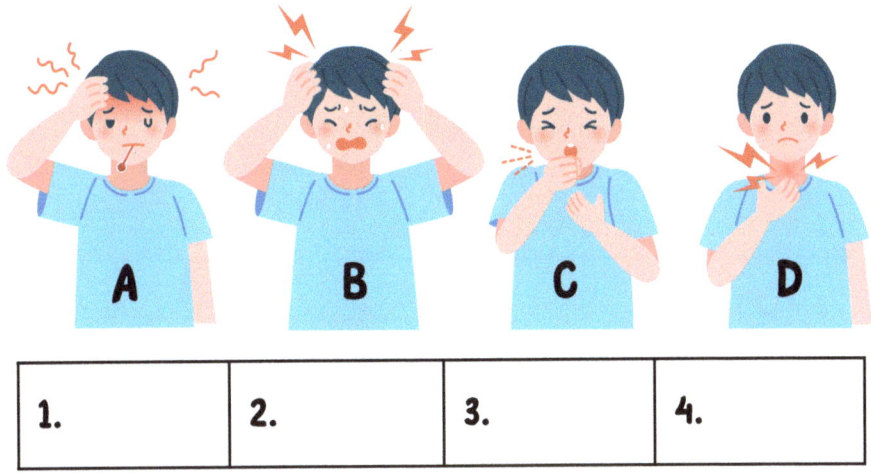

A **B** **C** **D**

1.	2.	3.	4.

ANSWERS:

C 1. A: What's the matter?   B: I have a cough.

A 2. A: What is the problem?   B: I have a fever.

D 3. A: What is wrong?   B: I have a sore throat.

B 4. A: Are you okay?   B: No. I have a headache.

LISTENING - School Supplies

Listen. Match pictures and sentences. Write the letters A, B, C, D inside the box.

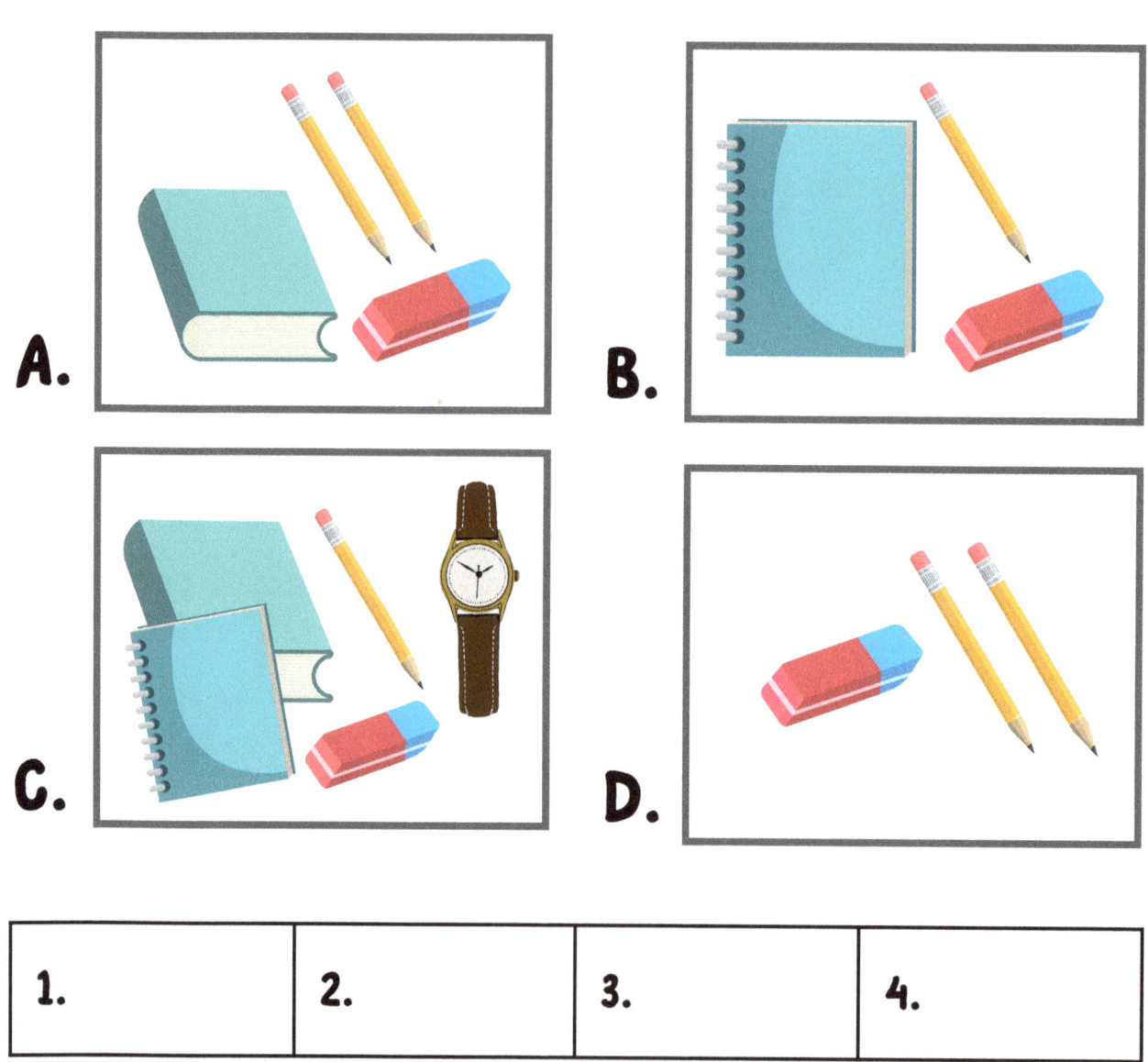

1.	2.	3.	4.

LISTENING - *School*

Listen. Match pictures and sentences. Write the letters A, B, C, D inside the box.

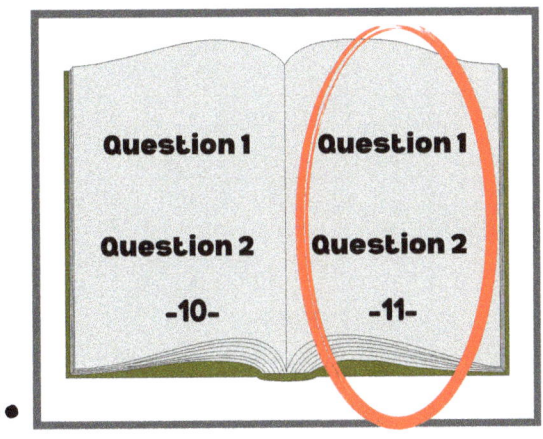

A.

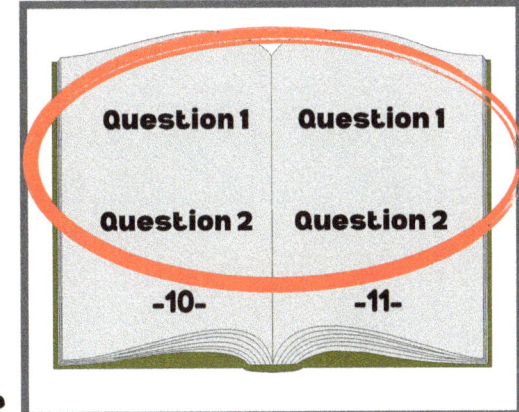

B.

C.

D.
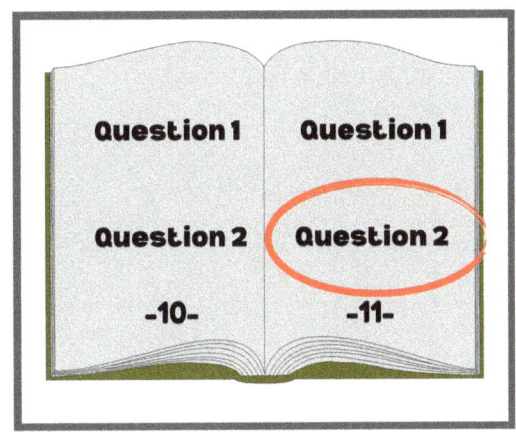

1.	2.	3.	4.

Listen. Match pictures and sentences. Write the letters A, B, C, D inside the box.

A.

B.

C.

D.

1.	2.	3.	4.

ANSWERS:
A 1. I help students learn in school.
D 2. I cook delicious food in a restaurant.
B 3. I make people healthy when they are sick.
C 4. I help with legal problems and speak in court.

Listen. Match pictures and sentences. Write the letters A, B, C, D inside the box.

A.

B.

C.

D.

1.	2.	3.	4.

Listen. Match places and sentences. Write the words inside the box.

1.	2.	3.	4.
5.	6.	7.	8.

ANSWERS:

school   1. I study in this place.
cafe   2. I drink my coffee in this place.
bank   3. I go to this place to get money.
hospital   4. I go to this place to visit a doctor.
fire station   5. This building is next to the church.
pool   6. This body of water is near the school.
grocery   7. This building is on the right of the city hall.
city hall   8. This building is between the pet shop and the grocery store.

Listen. Match pictures and sentences. Write the letters A, B, C, D inside the box.

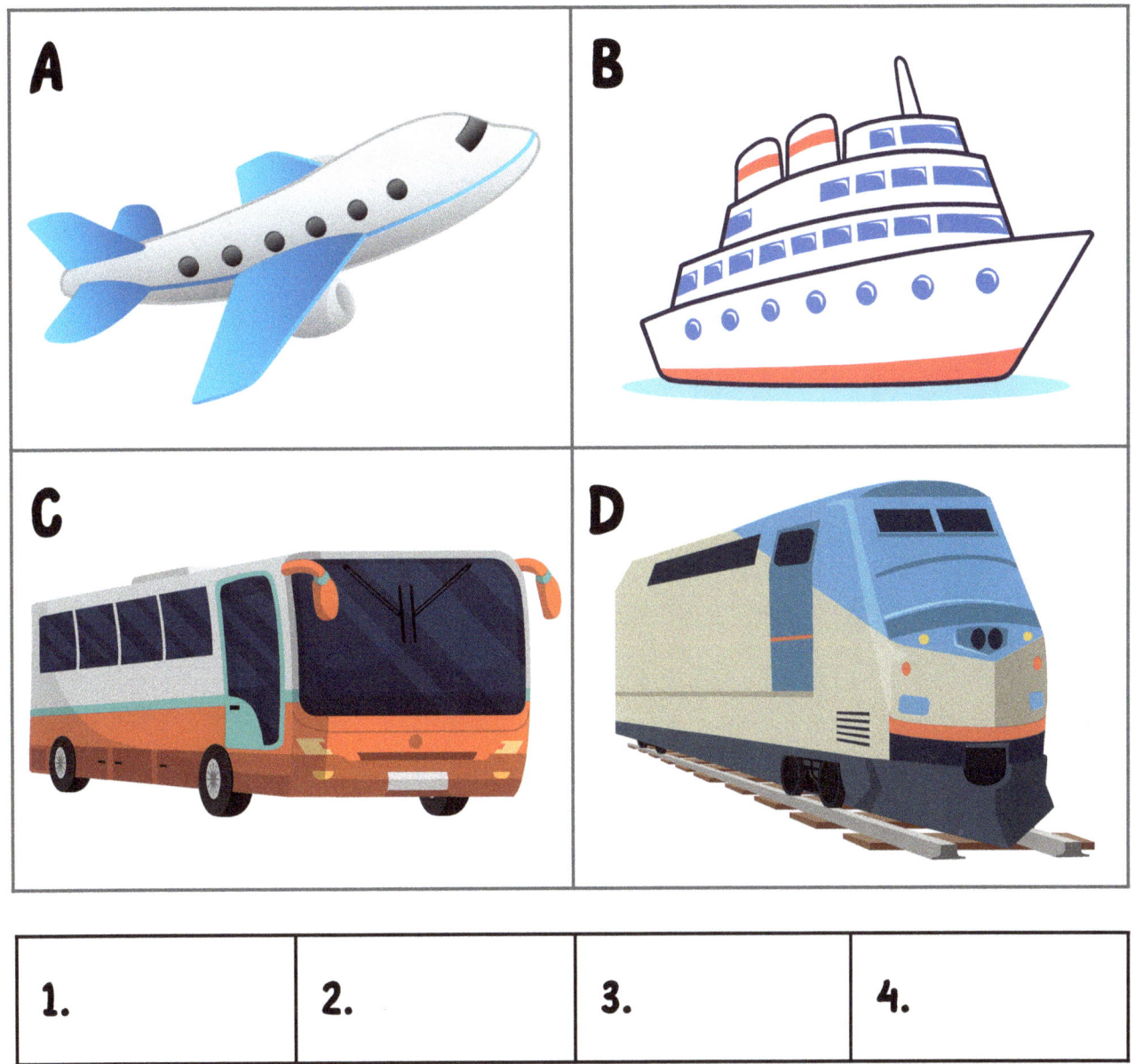

1.	2.	3.	4.

LISTENING - Money

Listen to the conversations. Match pictures and sentences. Write the letters A, B, C, D inside the box.

1.	2.	3.	4.

ANSWERS:

B 1. A: Hello! Can I help you?
B: Yes, please. I'd like to buy a handkerchief with a sunflower.
A: Which handkerchief would you prefer, the one with one sunflower or three sunflowers?
B: Just one sunflower, please.
A: Okay.

A 2. A: Hello! Can I help you?
B: Yes, do you have a handkerchief for one dollar?
A: Yes, we do.

D 3. A: Hello! Can I help you?
B: Yes, how much is this handkerchief?
A: It's twenty dollars.

C 4. A: Hello! Can I help you?
B: Yes, how much is this handkerchief with a red flower on it?
A: It's five dollars.
B: Is this the cheapest?
A: No, we have a handkerchief with a pink flower on it for one dollar.
B: I see. I'll take the one for five dollars.

Listen. Match pictures and sentences. Write the letters A, B, C, D, E, or F inside the box.

A. **B.** **C.**

D. **E.** **F.**

1.	2.	3.	4.

ANSWERS:

A. 1. I like this blue bag.

D. 2. I will buy this yellow backpack for my sister.

C. 3. I need a new bag. The green bag looks nice, but I'll buy the red one today.

E. 4. For my trip next week, I should buy this pink luggage because the orange suitcase is small.

LISTENING - Sports

Listen. Match pictures and sentences. Write the letters A, B, C, D inside the box.

1.	2.	3.	4.

Listen. Match pictures and sentences. Write the letters
A, B, C, D inside the box.

1.	2.	3.	4.

READING
AND
WRITING

READING - Weekly Schedule

Time	Monday	Tuesday	Wednesday	Thursday	Friday	Saturday	Sunday
5:00 - 5:30 AM	wake-up, prepare for work	wake-up, prepare for work	wake-up, prepare for work	wake-up, prepare for work	wake-up, prepare for work		
5:30 - 6:00 AM	breakfast	breakfast	breakfast	breakfast	breakfast	cook breakfast	cook breakfast
6:00 - 7:00 AM			work			breakfast	breakfast
7:00 - 8:00 AM	work						
8:00 - 11:00 AM	work	work			work		
11:00 AM- 12:00 PM		work		work	work		
12:00 - 1:00 PM		work		work	work		
1:00 - 5:00 PM		work			work		
6:00 - 8:50 PM	study	study	study	study	dinner	dinner, family time	dinner, family time
8: 50 - 10:00 PM	dinner, family time	dinner, family time	dinner, family time	dinner, family time			

This is Tina's weekly schedule:

Every weekday, Tina wakes up at 5 am. She eats breakfast at 5:30 am. She works every Monday to Friday. Also, she studies online every Monday to Thursday from 6 to 8:50 pm. After class, she eats dinner and spends time with her family. Tina does not work on weekends. On her days off, she stays home to take care of her three children, cooking for her family and enjoying their company.

Answer the questions. Circle the correct answers.

1. What time does Tina wake up every weekday?
a) 5 am
b) 6 am
c) 7 am

2. What time does Tina eat breakfast on Sunday?
a) 5:30 am
b) 6 am
c) 7 am

3. On which days does Tina study?
a) Monday to Friday
b) Monday to Thursday
c) Tuesday and Thursday

4. What does Tina do on weekends?
a) study
b) work
c) stay home

5. What time does Tina work on Monday?
a) 6 am – 8 am
b) 8 am – 5 pm
c) 7 am – 12 pm

READING - Household Expenses

Household Expenses

	Groceries	$200
	Housing (Rent/Mortgage)	$1, 200
	Utilities (Electricity, Water, Gas)	$150
	Transportation (Gas, Public Transit)	$100
	Healthcare (Insurance, Medications)	$50
	Education (School Fees, Supplies)	$30
	Entertainment (Dining out, Movies)	$100
	Miscellaneous (Clothing, Household Items)	$50
	Savings	$100

Answer the questions. Circle the correct answers.

1. How much money is for buying food in the budget?
a) $100
b) $150
c) $200
d) $1,200

2. Which part of the budget pays for your home, like rent or mortgage?
a) Housing
b) Groceries
c) Miscellaneous
d) Transportation

3. How much money is for having fun, like going out and watching movies?
a) $30
b) $50
c) $100
d) $150

4. What money is for taking care of your health, including insurance and medicines?
a) $50
b) $100
c) $200
d) $1,200

5. If you want to save $100, where in the budget should you put it?
a) Savings
b) Utilities
c) Education
d) Entertainment

ANSWERS: 1. c 2. a 3. c 4. a 5. a

USING A FIRE EXTINGUISHER
REMEMBER "PASS"

PULL THE PIN

Hold the extinguisher with the nozzle pointing away. Pull the pin at the top to unlock it.

AIM AT THE BASE

Point the nozzle at the bottom of the fire, not the flames. This is where the fire starts.

SQUEEZE THE HANDLE

Squeeze the handle to let out the foam. Hold the extinguisher firmly.

SWEEP FROM SIDE TO SIDE

Move the nozzle from side to side to cover the whole fire base. Keep a safe distance

IF THE FIRE DOESN'T GO OUT OR BECOMES TOO LARGE, EVACUATE AND CALL 911

Answer the questions. Circle the correct answers.

1. What is the first step?
a) Pull the pin
b) Aim at the base.
c) Squeeze the handle.
d) Sweep from side to side.

2. What do you do after pulling the pin?
a) Sweep the nozzle
b) Squeeze the handle
c) Evacuate and call 911
d) Aim at the base of the fire

3. Where to aim the nozzle?
a) Walls
b) Flames
c) Ceiling
d) Base of the fire

4. What to do while sweeping?
a) Close eyes
b) Stand still
c) Aim at flames
d) Maintain distance

5. What will you do if the fire is too large?
a) Evacuate
b) Squeeze again
c) Sweep faster
d) Aim at the ceiling

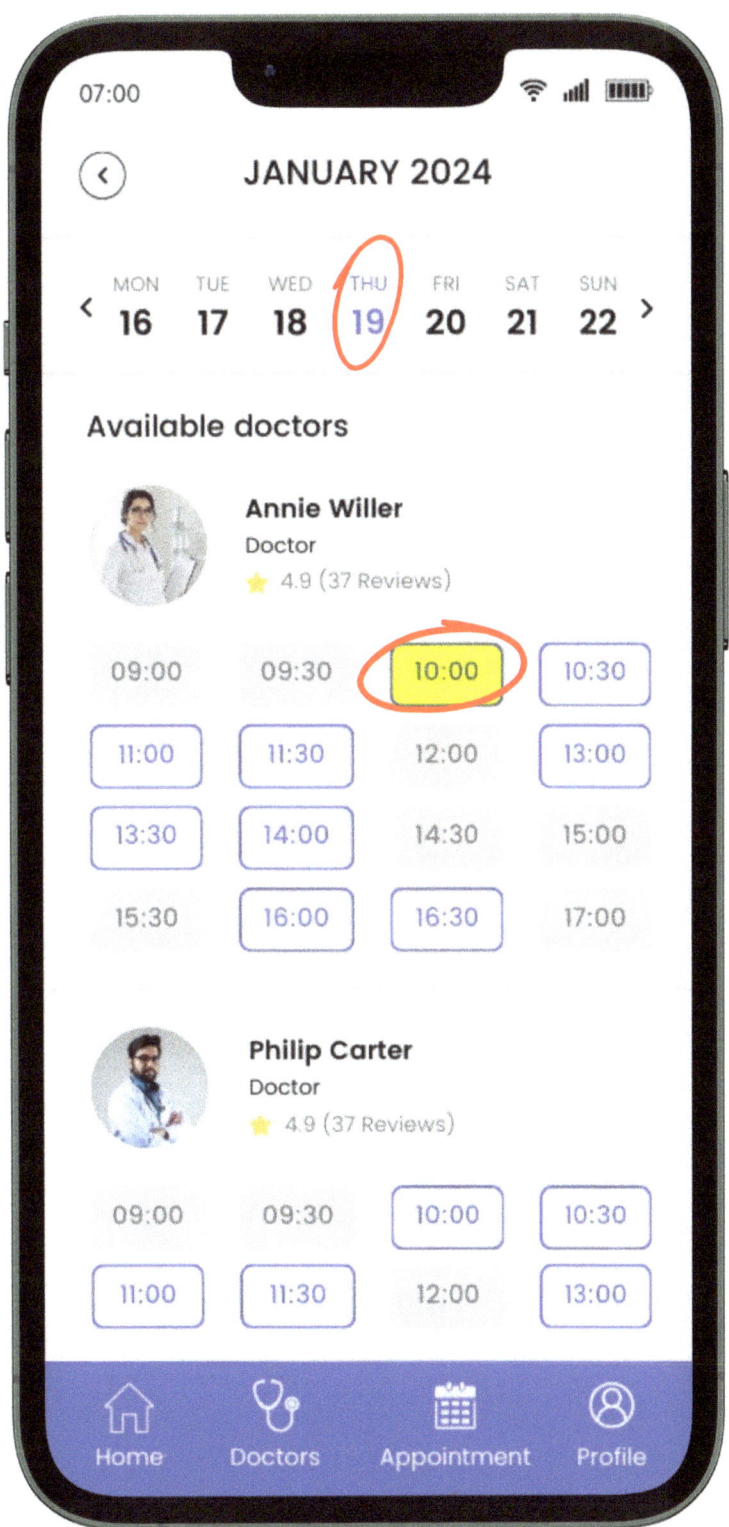

Answer the questions. Circle the correct answers.

1. What is the date of the appointment?
a) January 18, 2024
b) January 19, 2024
c) January 20, 2024

2. Which day of the week is the appointment?
a) Monday
b) Tuesday
c) Thursday

3. At what time is the appointment with Dr. Annie Willer?
a) 10:00
b) 11:00
c) 13:00

4. How many doctors are available for appointments at 10 am?
a) one
b) two
c) three

5. What is the latest available appointment time for Dr. Philip Carter on that day?
a) 10:00
b) 13:00
c) 16:30

Pain Reliever
Active ingredient: Acetaminophen 500 mg
Relieves: headache, aches and pain, fever

Directions
-Adults and children 12 years and over
-Take 2 tablets every 6 hours
-Do not take more than 8 tablets in 24 hours

Expiration Date: 8/2024

Match the questions and answers. Write the LETTER.

1. ___ How much do I take?
2. ___ What is the medicine for?
3. ___ Who can take the medicine?
4. ___ Who cannot use this product?
5. ___ What is the expiration date?

a. August 2024
b. children under 12
c. 2 tablets every six hours
d. adults and children over 12
e. headache, aches and pain, fever

Read and answer the questions.

William Tacker, M.D.
Seattle Washington Clinic
2625 First Avenue, WA 98106

Name: Anna Scott   **Age:** 39
Address: 1767 University Street
Seattle, WA 98121

Date: 04/03/2023

Cetirizine 10 MG

Signature: *William Tacker*

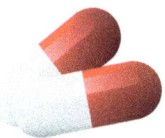

WALNUTT Pharmacy
Doctor: William Tacker
Patient: Anna Scott
Dosage: Take 1 tablet once a day. Take with food
Warning: Do not take while pregnant.

Cetirizine 10 MG
Exp: 08/27/ 2024

1. Who wrote the prescription?
_____

2. Who is it for?
_____

3. Where can you get this medicine?
_____

4. Who cannot use this product?
_____

5. What is the dosage?
_____

6. What is the name of the medicine?
_____

ANSWERS:1. c 2. e 3. d 4. b 5. a
1. Dr. William Tacker 2. Anna Scott 3. WALNUTT Pharmacy 4. pregnant 5. 1 tablet 6. Cetirizine

143

School Announcement for ESL 1 Students

📅 First Day of Online Class: Wednesday, September 27, 2023

🕐 Class Time: 6:00 pm - 8:50 pm

📚 Course Information

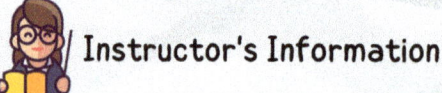 Days: MoTuWeTh (100% remote)
Class Dates: September 27, 2023 - December 14, 2023

👩‍🏫 Instructor's Information

Teacher: Geraldine Woods
✉️ Email: Geraldine.Woods@seattleschools.edu
📞 ESL Office Telephone: (206) 123-4567

Join us for a fantastic Fall quarter at Seattle School! ✨

Answer the questions. Circle the correct answers.

1. When is the first day of online class?
a) On September 26, 2023
b) On September 27, 2023
c) On September 28, 2023
d) On September 30, 2023

2. What time will the online class start?
a) At 6:50 in the morning
b) At 8:00 in the evening
c) At 8:50 in the evening
d) At 6:00 in the evening

3. On which days will students study?
a) Only on Monday and Tuesday
b) On Monday, Tuesday, and Thursday
c) On Monday, Tuesday, and Wednesday
d) On Monday, Tuesday, Wednesday, and Thursday

4. Who is the teacher for the class?
a) 100%
b) ESL Office
c) Seattle School
d) Geraldine Woods

5. In which quarter is the online class starting?
a) Fall quarter
b) Spring quarter
c) Winter quarter
d) Summer quarter

-ESL class meets Monday to Thursday from 6:00 - 8:50 pm

-The dance class meets every Friday from 1:00 - 2:00 pm.

-The teachers' meeting is every first Saturday of the month from 10:00 - 11:00 am

April						
Sun	Mon	Tue	Wed	Thu	Fri	Sat
						1
2	3	4	5	6	7	8
9	10	11	12	13	14	15
16	17	18	19	20	21	22
23	24	25	26	27	28	29
30	31					

True or False. Circle the correct answer.

1. The ESL class meets in the evening.   True   False

2. The dance class meets once a week.   True   False

3. The dance class meets in the morning.   True   False

4. The ESL class meets five days a week.   True   False

5. The teachers' meeting is once a month.   True   False

6. The teachers' meeting is on the weekend.   True   False

ANSWERS:1.True 2.True 3.False 4.False 5.True 6.True

Secretary Position

Requirements:
High school graduate

Age 18 and above

No work experience needed

Lives in Washington State

Job Description:
Answering phones

Scheduling appointments

Join our team as a Secretary!

Apply at our Main Office at

123 Pine Street Seattle, WA 98101.

Answer the questions. Circle the correct answers.

1. What do you need for this job?
a) ID
b) Driver's license
c) College diploma
d) High school diploma

2. How old should you be for this job?
a) 10 and above
b) 15 and above
c) 18 and above
d) 21 and above

3. Do you need work experience for this job?
a) No
b) Yes
c) Maybe
d) Only if you are old

4. In which state should you live for this job?
a) Seattle
b) Answering phones
c) Age 18 and above
d) Washington State

5. How do you apply for this job?
a) send an email
b) answer the phone
c) schedule an appointment
d) apply at the main office

November 11, 2023 ⟶ date

123 Elm Street
Smalltown, NY, 12345 ⟶ sender's address
alliesmith@email.com ⟶ sender's email address

Mr. Noa Johnson ⟶ receiver's name
Best Bargain Mart
456 Main Street
Smalltown, NY, 54321 ⟶ receiver's address

Dear Mr.Johnson, ⟶ receiver

My name is Allie Smith. I want to work at Best Bargain Mart. I am excited to help in your store. I can help customers. I can keep things clean. I can use the cash register. I like to learn and work with others. I am a good team member. Please consider me. Thank you.

Sincerely,

Allie Smith ⟶ writer / sender's signature

Answer the questions. Circle the correct answers.

1. What is the writer's name?
a) Ellie Smith
b) Allie Smith
c) Emma Smith

2. Where does Allie want to work?
a) at a school
b) at a store
c) at a restaurant

3. What can Allie do in the store?
a) cook food
b) fix computers
c) help customers

4. What is Mr. Noa Johnson's street address?
a) 123 Elm Street, Smalltown, NY, 12345
b) 456 Main Street, Smalltown, NY, 54321
c) None of the Above

5. How can Mr. Johnson contact Allie?
a) By sending an email
b) By calling her on the phone
c) By working at Best Bargain Mart

READING - Email

To: katiesullivan@gmail.com   →   receiver

From: alexanderson @gmail.com   →   sender / writer

Subject: Important - August 30th Kevin's Birthday Party Preparation

Hello Katie,

Please come to work at 8 am on Friday, August 30th, for our special birthday party setup. The party will begin at 10 am. Don't forget to wear Hawaiian clothes to match the theme. Your help is important to make this celebration fantastic!

Best regards,
Alex

Answer the questions. Circle the correct answers.

1. When is the special birthday party?
a) Friday, August 13th   b) Friday, August 30th

2. What time does the party begin?
a) 8 am   b) 10 am

3. What should Katie wear to the party?
a) Formal clothes   b) Hawaiian clothes

4. Who sent the email about the birthday party?
a) Alex   b) Katie

5. Why does Alex need help to set up the party?
a) To match the theme   b) To make the celebration fantastic

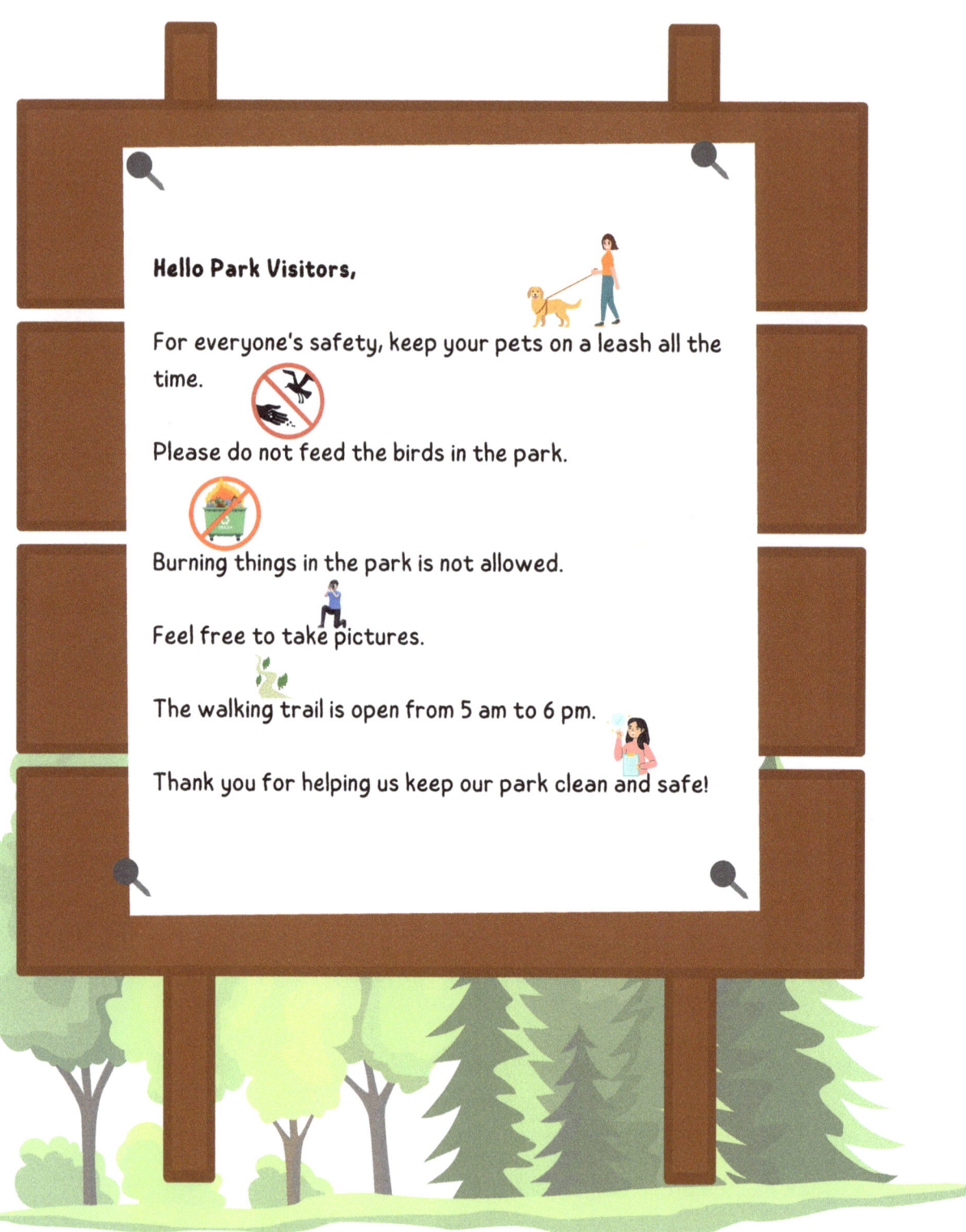

Hello Park Visitors,

For everyone's safety, keep your pets on a leash all the time.

Please do not feed the birds in the park.

Burning things in the park is not allowed.

Feel free to take pictures.

The walking trail is open from 5 am to 6 pm.

Thank you for helping us keep our park clean and safe!

Answer the questions. Circle the correct answers.

1. What should you do to keep the park safe?
a) Take pictures
b) Feed the birds
c) Burn things in the park
d) Keep your pets on a leash

2. What is not allowed in the park?
a) Burning things
b) Feeding the birds
c) Both a and b
d) None of the above

3. What time does the walking trail close?
a) 5 am
b) 6 am
c) 5 pm
d) 6 pm

4. What is okay to do in the park?
a) Burning leaves
b) Taking pictures
c) Feeding animals
d) Walking dogs without a leash

5. Why should you follow these rules in the park?
a) To feed the birds
b) To make the park dirty
c) To make other visitors angry
d) To keep the park clean and safe

READING - Road Signs

Road signs use different colors to give important information to drivers. Let's study some common colors and their meanings:

 **Red:** This color is for stop signs. It means drivers must stop.

 **Green:** This color shows directions, like the way to exits on highways.

 **Yellow:** Yellow signs warn drivers of danger ahead, such as curves or slippery roads.

 **Orange:** Orange signs are used in construction zones to alert drivers about road work.

 **Blue:** Blue signs are used for driver services and information, such as rest areas or tourist attractions.

Answer the questions. Circle the correct answers.

Question 1: Which color is used in construction zones?
a) blue   b) orange   c) green

Question 2: Which color is used for stop signs?
a) red   b) yellow   c) green

Question 3: What color is a sign for directions or guidance?
a) green   b) blue   c) orange

Question 4: What color is a sign that warn drivers of danger?
a) blue   b) orange   c) yellow

Question 5: What color is a sign that provide driver services and information?
a) red   b) green   c) blue

Bus Route from South Seattle College to Space Needle

Start at South Seattle College, located at 6000 16th Avenue SW, Seattle, WA.

Walk to the nearest bus stop.

Take Bus Route 120 towards Seattle Center.

Stay on the bus for 25 minutes.

Get off the bus at the Space Needle stop, and you will find yourself at the Space Needle!

Answer the questions. Circle the correct answers.

1.Where does the trip begin?
a) Space Center
b) Space Needle
c) South Seattle College
d) South Seattle Center

2. How do you go from South Seattle College to the bus stop?
a) fly
b) run
c) walk
d) drive

3. Which bus number should you take to get to the Seattle Center?
a) Bus 25
b) Bus 50
c) Bus 75
d) Bus 120

4. How many minutes should you stay on the bus?
a) 5 minutes
b) 10 minutes
c) 20 minutes
d) 25 minutes

5. Where should you get off the bus to reach the Space Needle?
a) Bus 120 stop
b) Space Needle stop
c) Space Center stop
d) South Seattle College stop

ANSWERS:1.c 2.c 3.d 4.d 5.b

READING - Boarding Pass Airline Ticket

Answer the questions. Circle the correct answers.

1. Where is William Darcy traveling from?

a) Florida   b) Texas   c) California   d) New York

2. What is the flight number for William Darcy's trip?

a) Flight 123

b) Flight 567

c) Flight AB 1234

d) Flight ABC1234

3. On which date is William Darcy's flight scheduled?

a) 9:00 AM   b) 22 August   c) AB 1234   d) ABC1234

4. What is the boarding time for the flight?

a) B 12   b) 9:00 AM   c) 9:00 PM   d) 22 August

5. Which class is William Darcy traveling in?

a) English   b) Economy   c) Business   d) First class

CityMart

Address: 123 College Street

Phone: (253) 111-1977

Receipt No: 123456

Date: 2023-09-21

Items Purchased:

Notebooks (5)	$6.99
Pens (10)	$3.49
Backpack	$19.99
Calculator	$12.99
Green Apples (8 lbs.)	$8.99
Shirt	$18.87
Subtotal	$71.32
Tax (7%)	$4.99
Total Amount	$76.31

Payment Method:Credit Card

Thank you for shopping at CityMart!

Answer the questions. Circle the correct answers.

1. Where is CityMart located?
a) $76.31
b) 111-1977
c) 2023-09-21
d) 123 College Street

2. How much do green apples cost?
a) $3.49
b) $4.99
c) $6.99
d) $8.99

3. What is the total amount spent at CityMart?
a) $4.99
b) $6.99
c) $71.32
d) $76.31

4. How much tax was paid on this purchase?
a) $4.99
b) 123456
c) 2023-09-21
d) (253) 111-1977

5. What was the payment method used for this purchase?
a) Address
b) Credit Card
c) Receipt Number
d) Items Purchased

READING - Shopping

Circle (True) if the sentence is correct ✓ and (False) if sentence is wrong ✗ .

1. The swimsuit size is large.   True   False

2. The swimsuit has an 8% discount.   True   False

3. The costumer's change is $3.80.   True   False

4. The swimsuit is $16.20 before tax.   True   False

5. The swimsuit is $15.00 after tax.   True   False

6. The date on the sales receipt is July 25, 2023.   True   False

SOUTH HILL

7/25/23

1 swimsuit (size M)	$30.00
Discount 50%	- 15.00
Subtotal	15.00
Sales Tax 8%	1.2
Total	16.20
CASH	20.00
Change	3.80

1. ___ Where is the sale?
2. ___ When is the sale?
3. ___ What are on sale?
4. ___ How much are the flip-flops on sale?

a. July 23-July 28
b. swimwear, sunglasses, and flip-flops
c. $3
d. North Hill Department Store

ANSWERS:1. False 2. False 3. True 4. False 5. False 6. True
1.d   2. a.   3. b   4. c

READING - Food and Restaurant Information

Read the milk's nutrition facts and answer the questions.

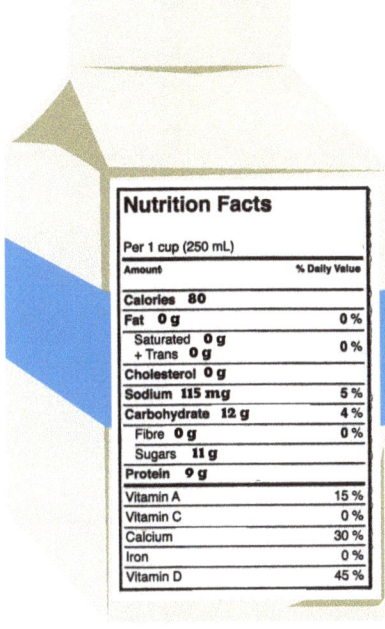

Nutrition Facts

Per 1 cup (250 mL)

Amount	% Daily Value
Calories 80	
Fat 0 g	0 %
Saturated 0 g + Trans 0 g	0 %
Cholesterol 0 g	
Sodium 115 mg	5 %
Carbohydrate 12 g	4 %
Fibre 0 g	0 %
Sugars 11 g	
Protein 9 g	
Vitamin A	15 %
Vitamin C	0 %
Calcium	30 %
Iron	0 %
Vitamin D	45 %

1. Does the milk have iron?

_____

2. Does the milk have sugar?

_____

3. What is 9 grams per serving?

_____

4. What vitamins are in the milk?

_____

5. How many calories does the milk have per serving?

_____

6. How many grams of fat does the milk have per serving?

_____

Answer the questions.

1. What is the name of the restaurant?

_____

2. Where is it located?

_____

3. When is it open?

_____

4. Is it open on Sundays?

_____

5. What time does the store close?

_____

6. Do they have a meal delivery service?

_____

Pizza With a Twist
Roosevelt, Seattle
DAILY 11 am - 11 pm
Dine-in or Take-out
For deliveries, call
253-269-8661

ANSWERS: 1. no 2. yes 3. 11 g 4. Vitamins A, C, and D 5. 80 6. 0
1.Pizza With a Twist 2. Roosevelt, Seattle 3. 11 am 4. yes 5. 11 pm 6. yes

161

SALAD MENU

HALAL حلال

"Healthy dishes for everyone"

SALAD WITH EGG $9

with Iced Green Tea or Lemonade

- - - - - - - - - - - - - - - - - - - -

Flavorful and Healthy

SALMON POKE BOWLS $25

with Coconut Water or Pineapple Juice

- - - - - - - - - - - - - - - - - - - -

A healthy taste of Hawaii

CHICKEN SALAD $15

with Iced Herbal Tea or Fresh Orange Juice

- - - - - - - - - - - - - - - - - - - -

Tender and juicy chicken breasts with light and flavorful salads.

DELIVERY: +123-456-7890 / www.saladdelights.com

Answer the questions. Circle the correct answers.

1. What is the menu?

a) Salad Menu

b) Healthy Bowls

c) Breakfast Specials

2. How much is the Chicken Salad?

a) $9

b) $15

c) $25

3. Which drink pairs with the "Salmon Poke Bowls"?

a) Iced Green Tea or Lemonade

b) Coconut Water or Pineapple Juice

c) Iced Herbal Tea or Fresh Orange Juice

4. Which salad is a healthy taste of Hawaii?

a) Chicken Salad

b) Salad with Egg

c) Salmon Poke Bowls

5. What is the website for Salad Delights?

a) www.saladdelight.com

b) www.saladheaven.net

c) www.saladdelicious.org

Spicy Chicken BBQ Recipe

Ingredients:

4 chicken breasts

1 cup BBQ sauce

2 tablespoons hot sauce

salt and pepper

cooking oil

Recipe:

Step 1: Put salt and pepper on the chicken.

Step 2: Mix BBQ sauce and hot sauce together in a bowl. This makes the spicy sauce.

Step 3: Pour the spicy sauce on the chicken. Wait for 10 minutes.

Step 4: Heat a pan or grill with some cooking oil. Put the chicken on it. Cook for about 10 minutes on each side until it is done.

Step 5: Take the chicken off the heat. Let it cool for a bit, then eat it with rice or bread!

Answer the questions. Circle the correct answers.

1. What should you put on the chicken in Step 1?
a) ketchup
b) BBQ sauce
c) hot sauce
d) salt and pepper

2. What do you mix together in Step 2 to make the spicy sauce?
a) milk and sugar
b) soy sauce and vinegar
c) mustard and mayonnaise
d) BBQ sauce and hot sauce

3. How long do you wait after pouring the spicy sauce on the chicken in Step 3?
a) 5 minutes
b) 10 minutes
c) 15 minutes
d) 20 minutes

4. What do you need to heat in Step 4 before putting the chicken on it?
a) blender
b) toaster
c) pan or grill
d) microwave

5. How long do you cook the chicken on each side in Step 4?
a) 2 minutes
b) 5 minutes
c) 10 minutes
d) 20 minutes

Answer the questions. Circle the correct answers.

1. What is the advertisement?
a) Meat
b) Pizza
c) Spicy
d) Delicious

2. How much is the pizza?
a) $4
b) $10
c) $20
d) $40

3. When is FREE DELIVERY available?
a) Monday-Friday
b) Friday-Sunday
c) Monday-Saturday
d) Tuesday-Thursday

4. What time does FREE DELIVERY start?
a) 10 AM
b) 10 PM
c) 11 AM
d) 11 PM

5. Where can you find more information?
a) In a book
b) On the roof
c) In the fridge
d) at www.reallygreatsite.com

ANSWERS: 1.b 2.d 3.a 4.a 5.d

WRITING - My Daily Routine

What do you do every day? Write at least 5 sentences.

Every day, I wake up early. I take a train to school. I study English in school. I speak English with my friends. I go home. I eat lunch. I clean my house. I wash my clothes and cook dinner. I eat dinner. I do my homework. I watch TV. I go to bed.

Score

What do you do every day? Write at least 5 sentences.

Every day, I _____

_____

_____

_____

_____

_____

_____

_____

Score

WRITING - My refrigerator

What's in the fridge? Write below.

1. ....
2. ....
3. ....
4. ....

5. ....
6. ....
7. ....
8. ....

9. ....
10. ....
11. ....
12. ....

What's in your refrigerator? Write at least 10 words.

I have _____.
Write below.

1. ....

2. ....

3. ....

4. ....

5. ....

6. ....

7. ....

8. ....

9. ....

10. ....

Recipe: Chicken Lumpia

Step 1: Prepare the filling by cutting chicken into small pieces and chopping vegetables.

Step 2: Mix the chicken and vegetables together in a bowl.

Step 3: Take a lumpia wrapper and put a spoonful of the filling in the middle.

Step 4: Fold and roll the lumpia tightly.

Step 5: Fry the lumpia in hot oil until golden brown.

Your turn. Write the steps of a food recipe.

WRITING - My First Email

4 PARTS OF THE EMAIL

STEP 1 Write your name and short information

STEP 2 Write your problem - housing, employment, childcare, health care

STEP 3 Write your request - please give information, give advise

STEP 4 Write thank you

To: supporthub@coastlinecollege.edu ——→ receiver

From: Geraldine.Woods@gmail.com ——→ sender / writer

Subject: Job Assistance ——→ Why write an email?

Dear Support Hub Team, ——→ receiver

I'm Geraldine Woods, an ESL 1 student at Sealine College. I am unemployed and need help finding a job. I would appreciate any help you can provide.

Thank you for your time and assistance.

Respectfully,
Geraldine Woods ——→ writer

To:

From:

Subject:

WRITING - My Family Tree

Hello! I'm Geraldine. I'm from the Philippines. Today, I will talk about my family. My family has five members: my husband, three children, and me. My husband's name is Robert. He works for the US government. My children are Devine, 18 years old, Nicole, 16 years old, and Junior, five months old. My daughters are in high school. I love my family. That's all. Thank you!

Draw your family tree.

My Family Tree

My Family Tree

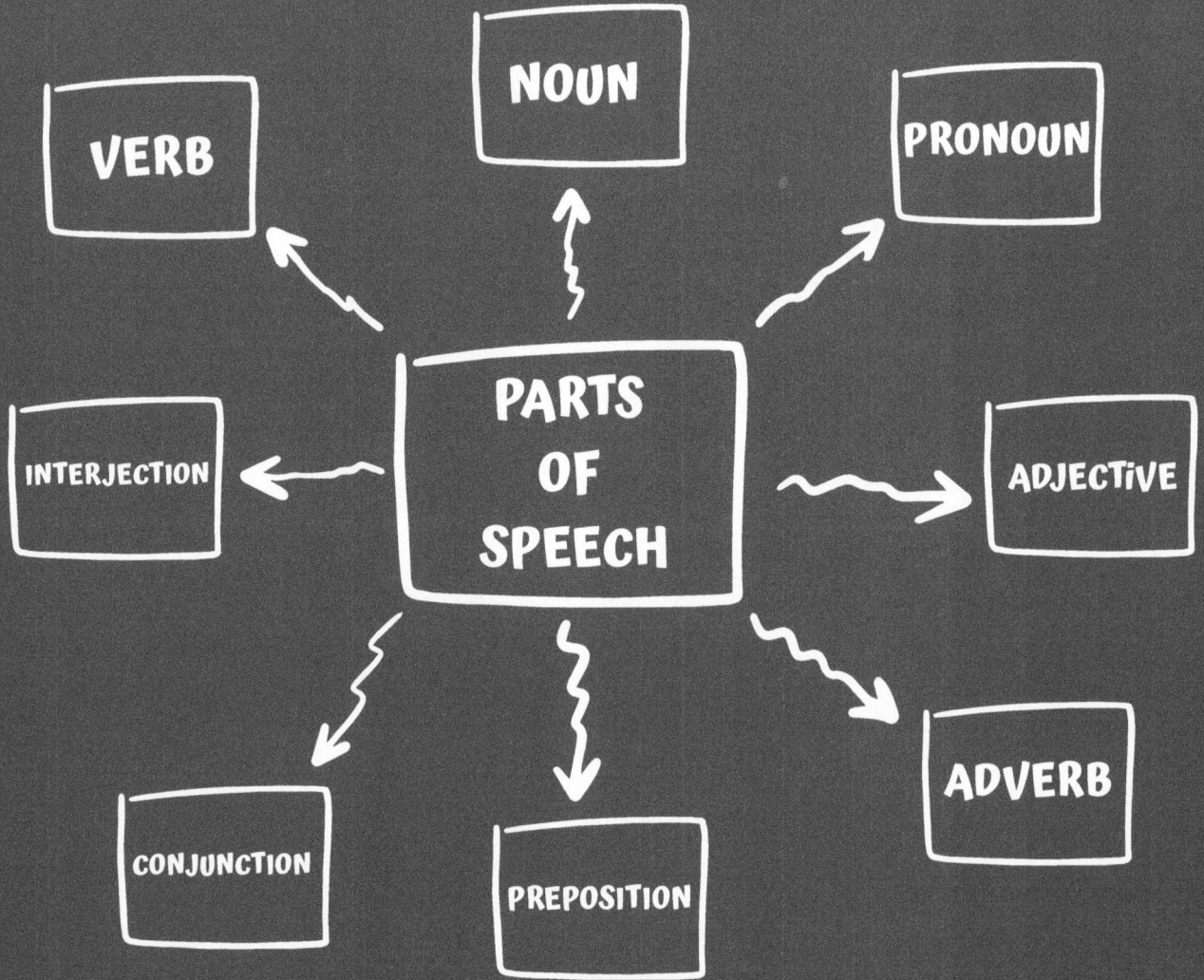

ENGLISH GRAMMAR

A NOUN is the name of a person, place, thing, animal, or event.

person

place

thing

animal

event

What noun is it? Circle the correct answer.

1.
person

place

2.
event

thing

3.
event

place

4.
animal

person

5.
animal

thing

6.
event

place

Indefinite Articles "a" " an"

If nouns begin with. a, e, i, o, u sounds, use "an" before them.

an apple

an egg

an igloo

an orange

an umbrella

a balloon

a cake

a door

a flag

a guitar

a hat

a jar

a kangaroo

a lemon

a mat

a nest

a pencil

a queen

a robot

a star

a tree

a vase

a wallet

a xylophone

a yoyo

a zoo

Use "an" before **vowels**

a, e, i, o, u

Use "a" before **consonants**

b, c, d, f, g, h, j, k, l, m, n, p, q, r, s, t, v, w, x, y, z

Be careful !

Beginning sounds are important. "u" in these nouns sounds as "y".

a unicorn

a university

When "h" is silent at the beginning of the noun, use "an"

an hour

an honor

Complete each sentence with "a" and "an."

1. It is _an_ egg.

2. It is____ door.

3. It is____ flag.

4. It is____ wallet.

5. It is ____ apple.

6. It is____ tree.

7. It is____ owl.

8. It is____ uniform.

9. It is____ ball.

10. It is____ car.

11. It is____ pot.

12. It is ____ ice cream.

Sight Word Sentences

Read and trace the sentences.

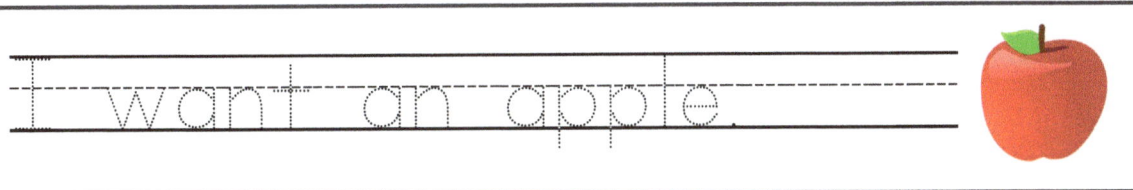

I want an apple.

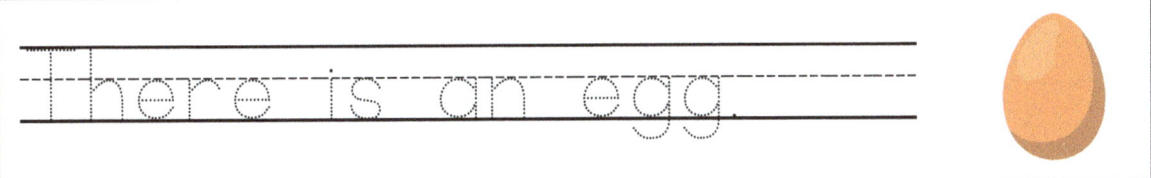

There is an egg.

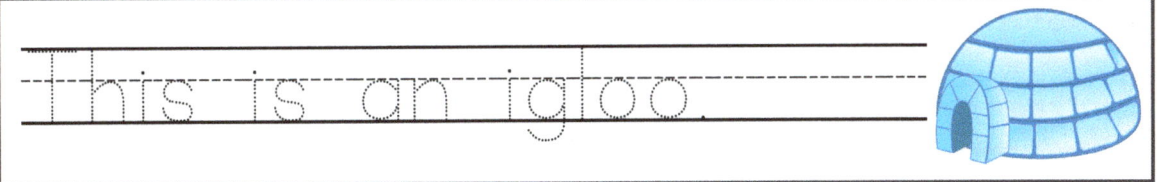

This is an igloo.

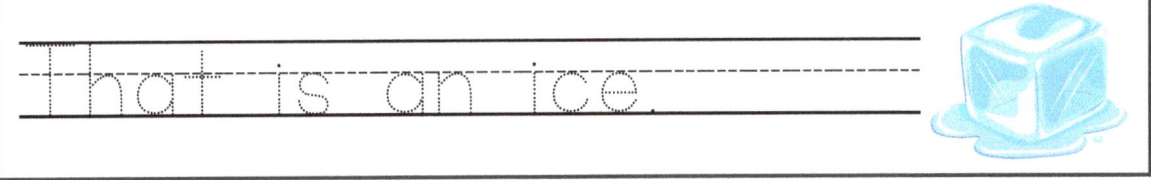

That is an ice.

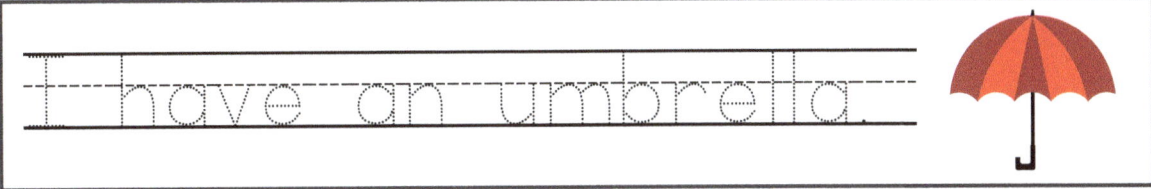

I have an umbrella.

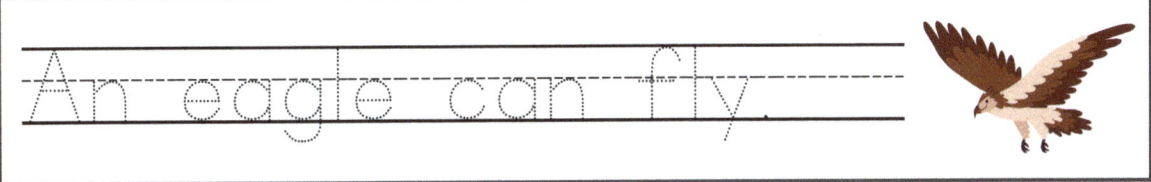

An eagle can fly.

I ride an elevator.

Sight Word Sentences

Read and trace the sentences.

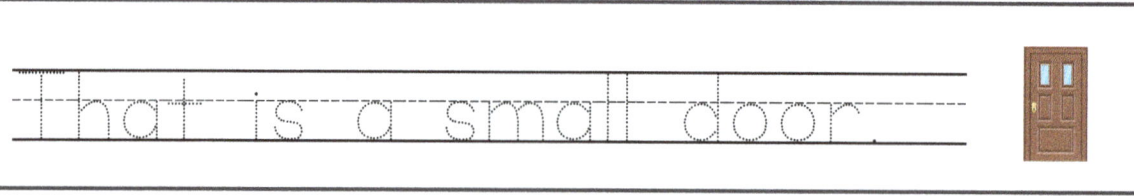

That is a small door.

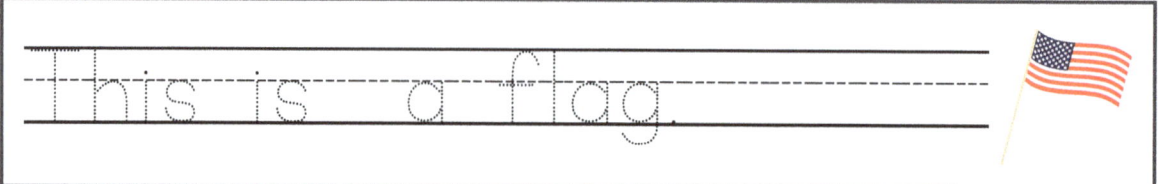

This is a flag.

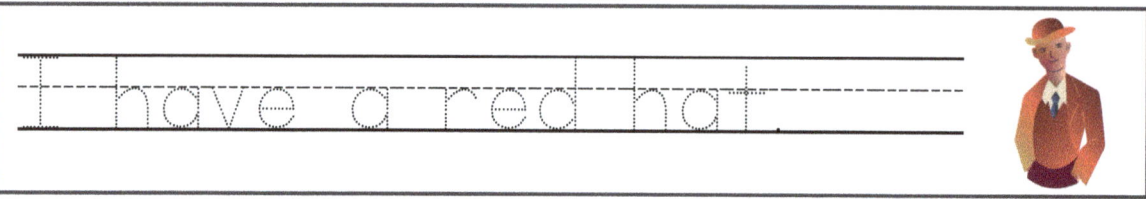

I have a red hat.

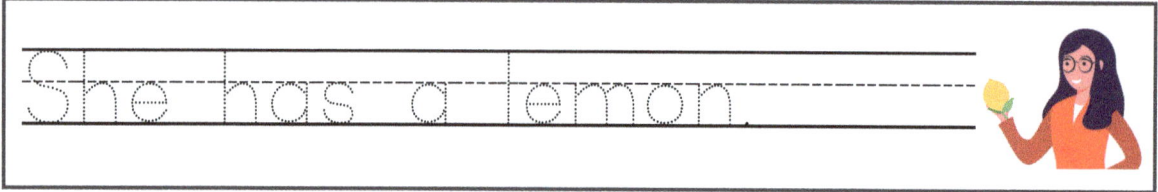

She has a lemon.

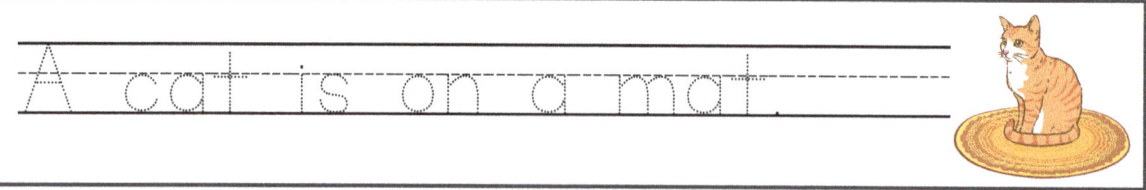

A cat is on a mat.

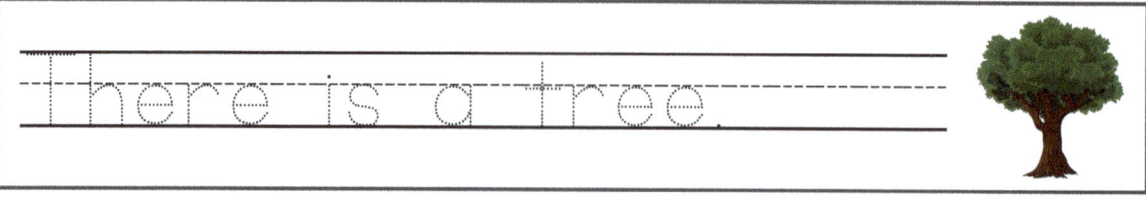

There is a tree.

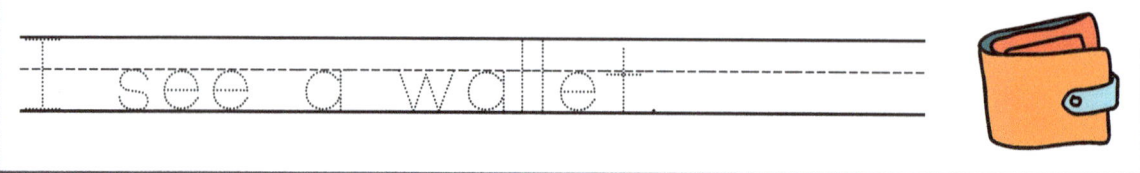

I see a wallet.

Sight Word Sentences

Read and trace the sentences.

This is the lion.

These are the lions.

The cow is eating.

The goat jumps high.

The ducks swim fast.

That is the ant.

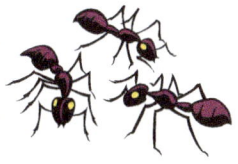

Those are the ants.

Plural Nouns

Regular Plural Nouns - add "s"

apple**s**

egg**s**

igloo**s**

orange**s**

umbrella**s**

balloon**s**

cake**s**

door**s**

flag**s**

guitar**s**

hat**s**

jar**s**

kangaroo**s**

lemon**s**

mat**s**

nest**s**

pencil**s**

queen**s**

robot**s**

star**s**

tree**s**

vase**s**

wallet**s**

xylophone**s**

yoyo**s**

zoo**s**

Plural Nouns RULES

Regular Nouns - add "s"

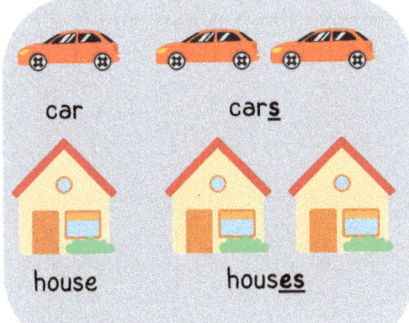

car   cars

house   houses

Ends in S, CH, SH, X, Z - add "es"

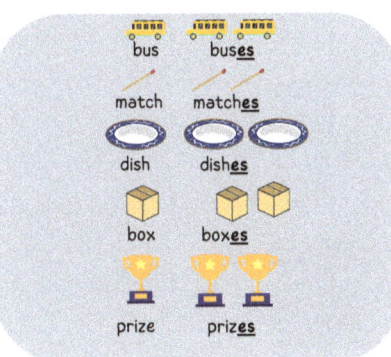

bus   buses

match   matches

dish   dishes

box   boxes

prize   prizes

Ends in F, FE - add "ves"

leaf   leaves

wolf   wolves

Ends in vowel + Y - add "s"

key   keys

boy   boys

Ends in consonant + Y - add "ies"

baby   babies

city   cities

Irregular Nouns

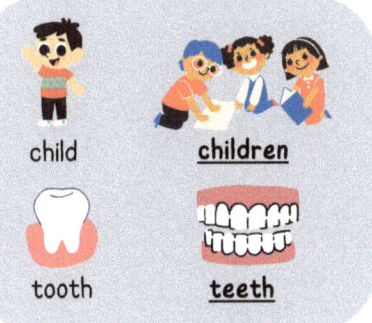

child   children

tooth   teeth

Ends in vowel + O - add "s"

radio   radios

kangaroo   kangaroos

Ends in consonant + O - add "es"

tomato   tomatoes

potato   potatoes

No change

sheep   sheep

deer   deer

What is the plural noun?

table		tables _____
glass		_____
shelf		_____
robot		_____
party		_____
man		_____
video		_____
hero		_____
luggage		_____

ANSWERS: glasses, shelves, robots, parties, men, videos, heroes, luggages

Proper and Common Nouns

common	Proper	
city	Seattle	
state	Washington	
country	United States of America	
day	Monday	
month	March	
school	South Seattle College	
car	Tesla	
movie	Spider-Man	
drink	Pepsi	
singer	Justin Bieber	

Choose: common or proper noun. Check the box.

noun	common	proper
1. Dr. John Smith		✔
2. August		
3. birthday		
4. book		
5. child		
6. dog		
7. Europe		
8. Hawaii		
9. mall		
10. Nike		
11. Saturday		

ANSWERS: 2. proper 3. common 4. common 5. common 6. common 7. proper 8. proper 9. common 10. proper 11. proper

A Pronoun takes the place of a noun.

Subject and Object Pronouns

I		me
you		you
he		him
she		her
it		it
we		us
they		them

Subject Pronouns

Look at the picture and circle the correct subject pronoun.

1. I
you

2. you
it

3. she
he

4. she
he

5. I
we

6. it
they

7. we
they

8. I
you

Subject Pronouns

The man
The father

He reads a newspaper.

He is reading a newspaper.

The woman
The mother

She cooks.

She cooks breakfast.

She is cooking.

She is cooking breakfast.

The children
The boy
and girl

They play.

They are playing.

The dogs
The pets
The animals

They eat.

They are eating.

Subject and Object Pronouns

(The man and the woman)

They give toys to **them**.
They give them toys.

(the family the woman and her children)

(The boy)

He gives a lollipop to **her**.
He gives her a lollipop.

(the girl)

(The girl)

She gives a doll to **her**.
She gives her a doll.

(another girl)

(The boy)

He gives a treat to **it**.
He gives it a treat.

(the dog)

(The woman)

She gives a present to **him**.
She gives him a present.

(the man)

Demonstrative Pronouns

<u>This</u> dress

<u>These</u> dresses

<u>That</u> dress

<u>Those</u> dresses

This **is** a dress.

- -

These **are** dresses.

- -

That **is** a dress.

- -

Those **are** dresses.

<u>This</u> sweater

<u>These</u> sweaters

<u>That</u> sweater

<u>Those</u> sweaters

This is a sweater.

These are sweaters.

That is a sweater.

Those are sweaters.

Circle the pictures that match the sentences.

	A	B
1. That is a bag.		
2. Those are diamonds.		
3. That is a sleeping baby.		
4. That is an old house.		
5. Those are laptops.		
6. Those are pens.		

Write <u>This is</u> or <u>These are</u> in each blank to complete the sentence.

1. _____ my shirt.

2. _____ my shoes.

3. _____ my pants.

4. _____ my coat.

5. _____ my socks.

6. _____ my cap.

A VERB is an action word.

bake	cross	give
breathe	cry	go
buy	dance	help
call	drink	hug
carry	drive	iron
choose	dry	laugh
clean	eat	listen
climb	exercise	mail
close	fasten	meet
cook	fold	open
count	get	pass

pay	rest	teach
play	ride	think
pray	run	turn
pull	sew	walk
push	shop	wash
put	shower	wait
sleep	sing	wake up
stop	sit	watch
study	smile	wear
read	stand	work
receive	talk	write

bake	cross	give
breathe	cry	go
buy	dance	help
call	drink	hug
carry	drive	iron
choose	dry	laugh
clean	eat	listen
climb	exercise	mail
close	fasten	meet
cook	fold	open
count	get	pass

pay	rest	teach
play	ride	think
pray	run	turn
pull	sew	walk
push	shop	wash
put	shower	wait
sleep	sing	wake up
stop	sit	watch
study	smile	wear
read	stand	work
receive	talk	write

"Be" Verbs - is, are ,was, were

RULE: past, singular - use "**was**"

The man **was** happy.

RULE: present, singular - use "**is**"

The man **is** happy.

RULE: past, plural - use "**were**"

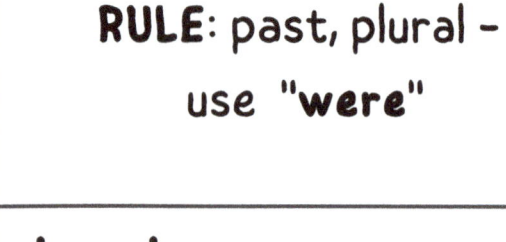

The women **were** sick.

RULE: present, plural - use "**are**"

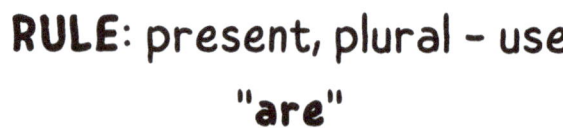

The women **are** sick.

Circle the correct answer.

1. I love going to the mall. The clothes (is am **are**) on sale.

2. This is the new library. The books (is am **are**) on those shelves.

3. Can you see me? I (is **am** are) here.

4. This is my brother. He (**is** am are) five years old.

5. Her name is Maleela, she (**is** am are) from my English class.

6. I got a new computer, it (**is** am are) the best!

Look at each person's ages and answer the questions using is - are - am.

Avery - 8   Rosa - 78   Soo - 8

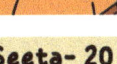

Francisco - 12   Seeta- 20   Samira - 20

Anna - 20   Sacha - 6   Taylor - 6

1. How old is Soo?

2. How old are Avery and Soo?

3. How old is Rosa?

4. How old is Francisco?

5. How old are Seeta and Samira?

6. How old are Sacha and Taylor?

7. How old are Anna and Seeta?

8. How old are you?

Subject + Verb Rule

RULE: present, singular subject + regular verb with -s

The boy plays soccer.

He plays soccer.

The girl plays basketball.

She plays basketball.

RULE: present, plural subject + regular verb no-s

The boys play soccer.

They play soccer.

The girls play basketball.

They play basketball.

RULE: I and YOU + verb no-s

 I play soccer.
 You play soccer.

 I play basketball.
 You play basketball.

RULE: past, singular subject + verb with -d / ed

The boy played soccer.

He played soccer.

The girl played basketball.

She played basketball.

RULE: past, plural subject + verb with -d / ed

The boys played soccer.

They played soccer.

The girls played basketball.

They played basketball.

RULE: I and YOU + verb with -d / ed

 I played soccer.
 You played soccer.

 I played basketball.
 You played basketball.

Verb Tense Rule

PAST yesterday	PRESENT now	FUTURE tomorrow
 The boy played.	 The boy plays.	 The boy will play.
 The boys played.	 The boys play.	 The boys will play.
 The boy was playing.	 The boy is playing.	 The boy will be playing.
 The boys were playing.	 The boys are playing.	 The boys will be playing.

Simple Tense (Singular Subject)

PAST yesterday	PRESENT today	FUTURE tomorrow
The man watched TV.	The man watches TV.	The man will watch TV.
The woman vacuumed the floor.	The woman vacuums the floor.	The woman will vacuum the floor.
The baby played with the ball.	The baby plays with the ball.	The baby will play with the ball.

Continuous/Progressive Tense (Singular Subject)

PAST yesterday	PRESENT today	FUTURE tomorrow
The man was watching TV.	The man is watching TV.	The man will be watching TV.
The woman was vacuuming the floor.	The woman is vacuuming the floor.	The woman will be vacuuming the floor.
The baby was playing with the ball.	The baby is playing with the ball.	The baby will be playing with the ball.

Simple Tense (Plural Subject)

PAST yesterday	PRESENT today	FUTURE tomorrow
The men watched TV.	The men watch TV.	The men will watch TV.
The women vacuumed the floor.	The women vacuum the floor.	The women will vacuum the floor.
The baby and the cat played with the ball.	The baby and the cat play with the ball.	The baby and the cat will play with the ball.

Continuous/Progressive Tense (Plural Subject)

PAST yesterday	PRESENT today	FUTURE tomorrow
The men were watching TV.	The men are watching TV.	The men will be watching TV.
The women were vacuuming the floor.	The women are vacuuming the floor.	The women will be vacuuming the floor.
The baby and the cat were playing with the ball.	The baby and the cat are playing with the ball.	The baby and the cat will be playing with the ball.

Simple Present Sentences

The baby and the cat play with the ball.

The woman vacuums the floor.

The man watches TV.

....

Present Progressive/Continuous Sentences

The baby and the cat are playing with the ball.

The woman is vacuuming the floor.

The man is watching TV.

What are they doing? Circle the correct answer.

1. He is resting / running.

2. They are walking / working.

3. They are waiting / washing.

4. She is driving a car / riding a bike.

5. He is reading / writing.

6. She is studying / watching TV.

ANSWERS: 1. resting 2. working 3. waiting 4. driving a car 5. writing 6. watching TV

REGULAR VERB TENSE

Present Tense	Past Tense	Past Participle	Future Tense
bake	baked	baked	will bake
clap	clapped	clapped	will clap
hug	hugged	hugged	will hug
jump	jumped	jumped	will jump
laugh	laughed	laughed	will laugh

Present Tense	Past Tense	Past Participle	Future Tense
open	opened	opened	will open
play	played	played	will play
shop	shopped	shopped	will shop
travel	traveled	traveled	will travel
watch	watched	watched	will watch

IRREGULAR VERB TENSE

Present Tense	Past Tense	Past Participle	Future Tense
bite	bit	bitten	will bite
blow	blew	blown	will blow
catch	caught	caught	will catch
cut	cut	cut	will cut
do	did	done	will do

Present Tense	Past Tense	Past Participle	Future Tense
give	gave	given	will give
go	went	gone	will go
make	made	made	will make
read	read	read	will read
run	ran	run	will run

Circle the pictures that match the sentences.

		A	**B**
1. I can read.			
2. I can run.			
3. I can jump.			
4. I can shop.			
5. I can play.			

has - have - had

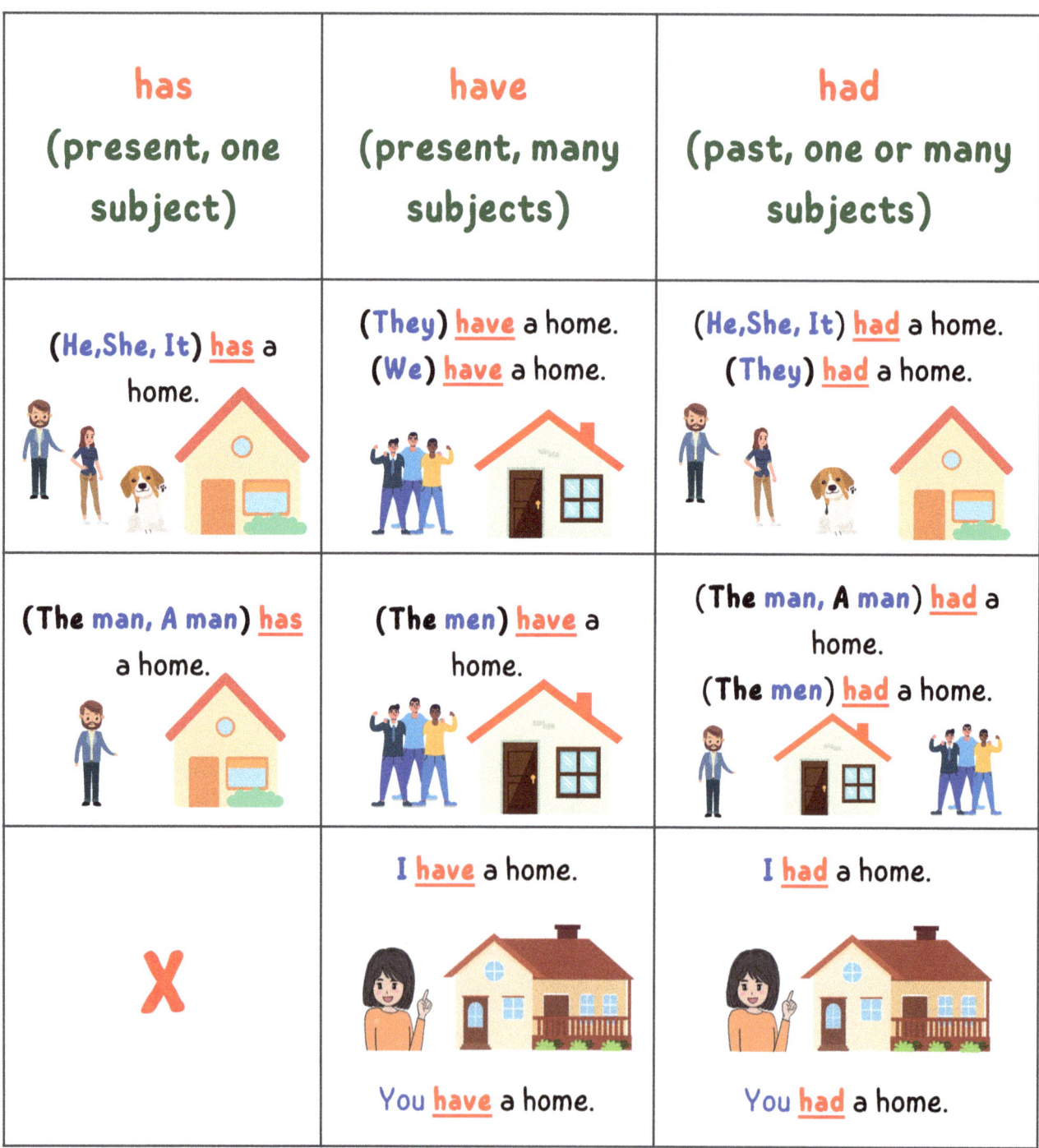

has (present, one subject)	have (present, many subjects)	had (past, one or many subjects)
(He, She, It) has a home.	(They) have a home. (We) have a home.	(He, She, It) had a home. (They) had a home.
(The man, A man) has a home.	(The men) have a home.	(The man, A man) had a home. (The men) had a home.
X	I have a home. You have a home.	I had a home. You had a home.

Write "has" or "have" to complete the sentences.

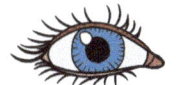

1. We _____ two eyes.

has	have

2. I _____ toys.

has	have

3. The fish _____ fins.

has	have

4. He _____ a car.

has	have

5. We _____ a home.

has	have

6. She _____ a new dress .

has	have

ANSWERS: 1. have 2. have 3. has 4. has 5. have 6. has

An ADJECTIVE describes a noun.

big elephant

busy woman

calm man

cold winter

fast driver

happy family

hot summer

long hair

loud music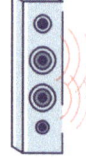

new shoes

old book

quiet nature

sad girl

short pants

small rat

slow cooker

tall tree

soft feather

tasty pie

Read and circle.

	A	**B**
1. a big dog		
2. a hot tea		
3. a new bag		
4. a soft blanket		
5. a small ball		
6. a happy child		
7. a short stairs		
8. a fast train		

Opposites

up down

hot

cold

close

open

happy

sad

on

off

old

new

full

empty

day

night

big

tall

soft

long

out

small

short

hard

short

in

slow

fast

young

old

stop

go

sunny

rainy

Let's Play Opposites

Answer the questions. Circle the correct answer.

1. What is the opposite of "hot"?

a) cold

b) close

c) open

2. What is the opposite of "happy"?

a) on

b) off

c) sad

3. What is the opposite of "big"?

a) short

b) small

c) tall

4. What is the opposite of "full"?

a) day

b) night

c) empty

5. What is the opposite of "slow"?

a) old

b) fast

c) young

ANSWERS: 1.a 2.c 3.b 4.c 5.b

Answer the questions.

1. What is the opposite of "tall"?

_____

2. What is the opposite of "new"?

_____

3. What is the opposite of "in"?

_____

4. What is the opposite of "stop"?

_____

5. What is the opposite of "sunny"?

_____

Adverbs of Frequency

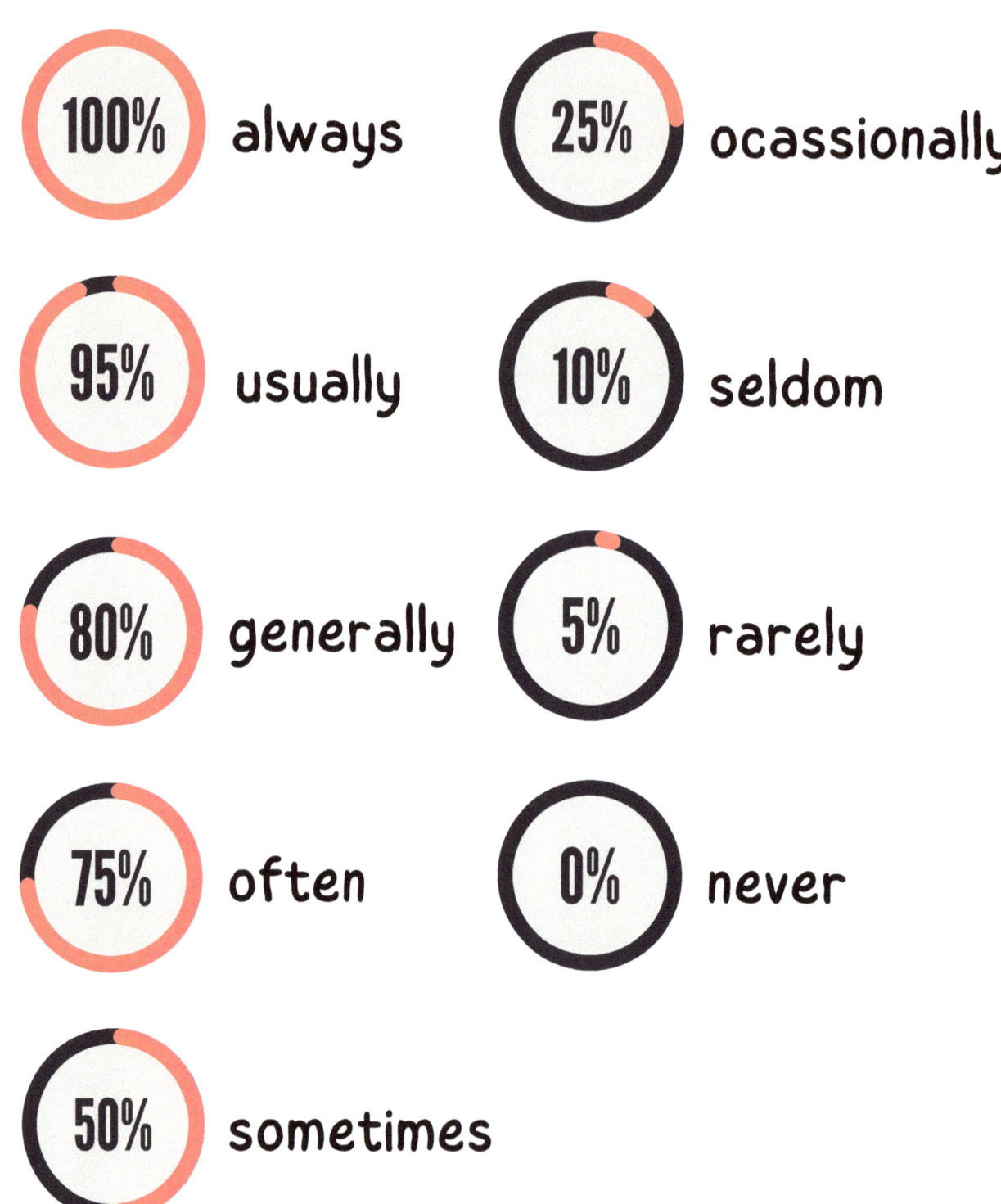

100% always

95% usually

80% generally

75% often

50% sometimes

25% ocassionally

10% seldom

5% rarely

0% never

These figures are approximations.

A. Look at the frequency of each sentence and choose the correct adverb.

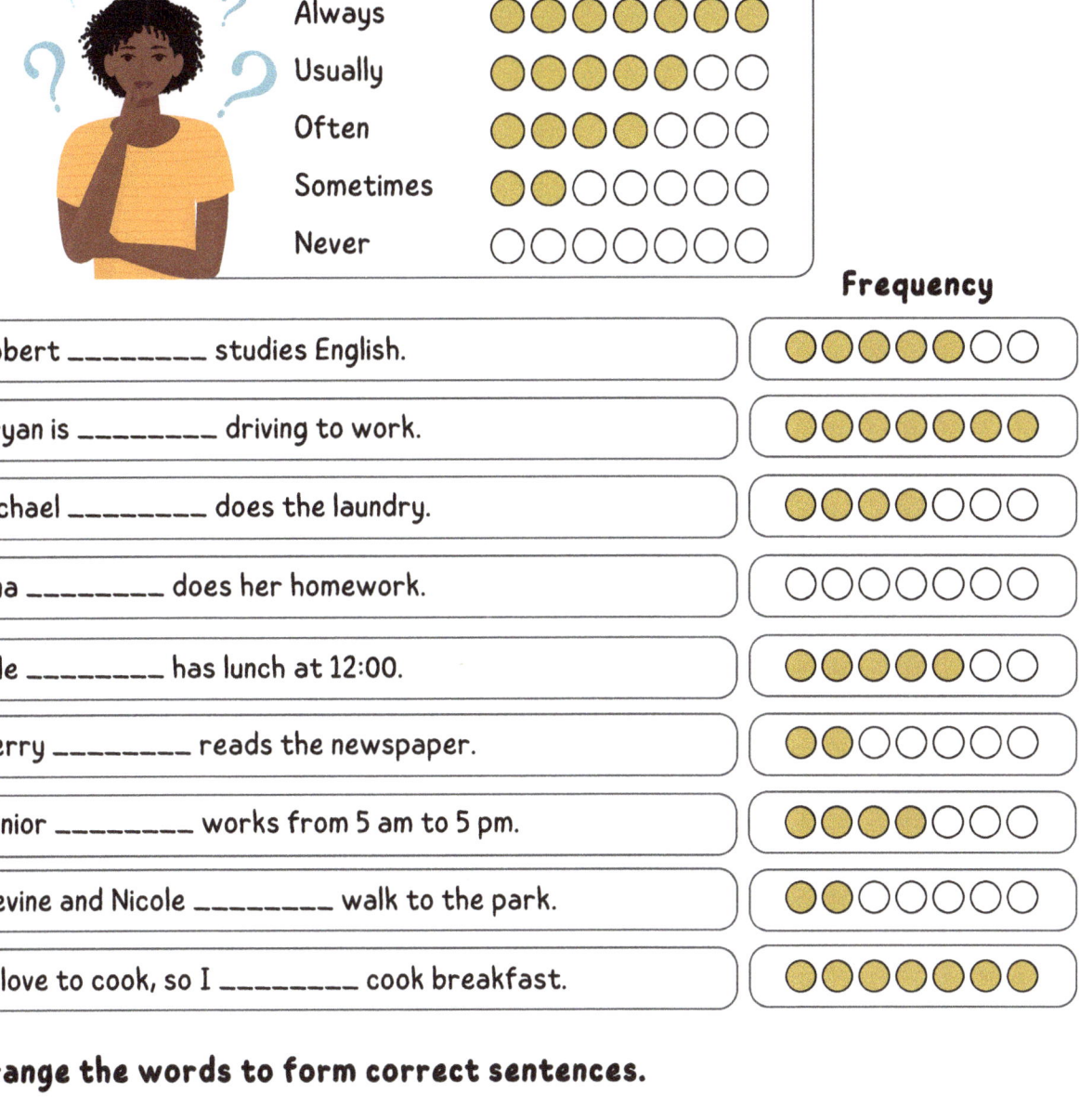

Always	●●●●●●●
Usually	●●●●●○○
Often	●●●●○○○
Sometimes	●●○○○○○
Never	○○○○○○○

Frequency

1. Robert _____ studies English. ●●●●●○○

2. Bryan is _____ driving to work. ●●●●●●●

3. Michael _____ does the laundry. ●●●○○○○

4. Ana _____ does her homework. ○○○○○○○

5. Kyle _____ has lunch at 12:00. ●●●●●○○

6. Terry _____ reads the newspaper. ●●○○○○○

7. Junior _____ works from 5 am to 5 pm. ●●●●○○○

8. Devine and Nicole _____ walk to the park. ●●○○○○○

9. I love to cook, so I _____ cook breakfast. ●●●●●●●

B. Arrange the words to form correct sentences.

1. never / i am / late / for classes / . _____

2. often / bob / goes / to the gym / . _____

3. always / andre / very friendly / is / . _____

4. usually / helps / in the kitchen / angie /. _____

5. sometimes / jenny / the floor / vacuums / . _____

Prepositions of Place

Where is the cat?

The cat is **in** the box.
The cat is **inside** the box.

The cat is **on** the chair.

The cat is **under** the table.

The cat is **in front of** the dog.

The cat is **at the back of** the dog.
The cat is **behind** the dog.

The cat is **by** the plant.
The cat is **near** the plant.
The cat is **beside** the plant.
The cat is **next to** the plant.
The cat is **close to** the plant.

The cat is **between** the bowls.

The cat is **on the right of** the bowl.

The cat is **on the left of** the bowl.

The cat is **straight** ahead.

The cat is **across from** the dog.

The cat is **up** the tree.

The cat is **down from** the tree.
The cat is **below** the tree.

Circle the letter if you see the school supplies in the picture.

Where is the _____?

A - The pen is on the desk.

B - The bag is in the desk.

C - The chair is by the desk.

D - The clock is on the wall.

E - The folder is in the globe.

F - The scissors are in the bag.

G - The books are on the table.

H - The eraser is by the pencil.

I - The notebook is on the bag.

J - The crayon is under the chair.

K - The sharpener is by the pencil

L - The pencil is in the pencil case.

M - The marker is under the table.

N - The notebook is under the chair.

O - The highlighter is by the laptop.

Prepositions of Time

at	on	in	from, to
9 am 4 pm 8 o'clock 6 in the afternoon	Sunday my birthday March 15th Thanksgiving	March 2023 the morning summer	9 am – 11 am 3 o'clock – 6 o-clock

He goes to church **on Sunday**.

He studies **from 9 am to 11 am**.

She eats breakfast **at 9 am**.

She celebrates her birthday **in March**.

1. I study _____ 6 pm.

2. I work _____ 6 pm _____ 8:50 pm.

3. The class starts _____ January.

4. I will go to the mall _____ Monday.

5. The weather is cold _____ winter.

ROLE-PLAY
and
CONVERSATIONS
Q and A

Staff: Hello! Welcome to **Pizza Twist**! May I take your order?

Customer: Yes. I'd like one chicken pizza, please.

Staff: Okay. What size is the chicken pizza?

Customer: Large, please.

Staff: How spicy? From 1 to 5, 5 is very spicy.

Customer: Make it 3.

Staff: Anything else?

Customer: Yes, I'd like a 1-liter Pepsi.

Staff: Got it. Anything else?

Customer: No, that's it.

Staff: Your total is $20. Will you pay with cash or a card?

Customer: Card, please.

Staff: Great. May I have the name on the card?

Customer: It's [say your name].

Staff: Your card number, please?

Customer: It's 4275 3156 0372 5493.

Staff: Thank you. The three-digit code on your card?

Customer: It's 452.

Staff: Great. What's the expiration date?

Customer: It's 01/29.

Staff: And for delivery, can I have your address and phone number?

Customer: My address is [say your complete address], and my phone number is [say your phone number].

Staff: Thank you for choosing Pizza Twist. Your order will be on its way. Enjoy your meal!

Customer: Thanks! Goodbye.

Staff: Goodbye, and have a great day!

customer   staff

ROLE-PLAY - Ordering at a Restaurant

Customer: Hello.

Waiter/Waitress: Hi there! Welcome to **Food Delight**. What would you like to eat?

Customer: May I have the rice and chicken?

Waiter/Waitress: Sure thing. Would you like something to drink?

Customer: Yes, just water, no ice, please.

Waiter/Waitress: Got it. Rice, chicken, and water, no ice. Is there anything else?

Customer: No, that's all, thank you.

Waiter/Waitress: Okay, I'll get that for you. Thanks!

Waiter/Waitress: Here's your chicken and rice and your water.

Customer: Thank you!

Waiter/Waitress: Enjoy your meal. If you need anything else, just let me know.

Customer: I will. Thanks!

ROLE-PLAY - Booking a Hotel Room

Receptionist: Hi! Welcome to Sun Hotel. How can I help you?

Customer: Hi, I want a room, please.

Receptionist: Okay. What's your name?

Customer: My name is [say your name].

Receptionist: Hi, [say the name]. When will you come to the hotel?

Customer: April 25th.

Receptionist: Got it. How many nights will you stay?

Customer: Three nights.

Receptionist: Alright. We have single and double rooms. Which one do you want?

Customer: Double room, please.

Receptionist: Sure thing. Only non-smoking rooms. Is that okay?

Customer: Yes, non-smoking is fine.

Receptionist: Perfect. Your reservation is set for a double non-smoking room from April 25th for three nights. Do you want breakfast or an extra bed?

Customer: No, just the room is okay.

Receptionist: Understood. Your room is $100 per night. What's your phone number and email to confirm?

Customer: My phone number is [say your phone number], and my email is [say your email address].

Receptionist: Thank you, [say the name]. We will send you an email. Anything else?

Customer: No, that's all. Thanks for your help.

Receptionist: You're welcome. See you on April 25th. Have a great day!

Customer: You too. Goodbye!

Allie: Excuse me, can you help me find the train station?

Noah: Of course. Which train station are you looking for?

Allie: King Street station.

Noah: It's close. First, go straight down this street.

Allie: Okay, straight down this street.

Noah: After two blocks, turn left there.

Allie: Turn left after two blocks. Got it.

Noah: Then, keep walking, and you will see the train sign. Follow that sign, and it will take you to the train station.

Allie: Thank you for your help.

Noah: You're welcome!

ROLE-PLAY - Going to the Doctor

In the Reception Area

Patient: Hi, I have a doctor's appointment today.

Receptionist: Sure, your name, please?

Patient: Ana Curtis.

Receptionist: Thanks, Ana. Your appointment is at 2:00 p.m. Fill out this form, please.

Patient: Here.

Receptionist: Great. Take a seat. The doctor will see you soon.

Patient: Thank you.

In the Doctor's Room

Doctor: Hi, Ana. How are you today?

Patient: I'm okay, just tired.

Doctor: Let's check your health. Roll up your sleeve for blood pressure.

Patient: Okay.

Doctor: Blood pressure is good. Now, open your mouth for a throat check.

Doctor: Everything looks fine. Any pain or discomfort?

Patient: No, I feel fine.

Doctor: Are you taking any medications?

Patient: No.

Doctor: Good. Eat well, exercise, and rest. If you feel unwell, come back.

Patient: Thanks, Doctor.

Doctor: You're welcome. Take care.

Beth: Hi, can you help me find a dress, please?

Amanda: Sure. What color do you like?

Beth: I like blue.

Amanda: Great! Please follow me. We have blue dresses over here.

Beth: How about that one?

Amanda: Nice choice! What size do you need?

Beth: I'm a medium.

Amanda: Let me check if we have it in a medium. Yes, we do! Here you go.

Beth: It looks good. How much is it?

Amanda: It's $30. Is that okay?

Beth: Yes, that's fine. I'll take it. Thank you for your help.

Amanda: You're welcome. Have a great day!

Amanda: You too!

ROLE-PLAY - Talking about Sports

Adam: Hey, what's your favorite sport?

Ben: Hi! I really like football. How about you?

Adam: Oh, I love playing baseball with my friends!

Ben: That sounds fun! What do you like about baseball?

Adam: Hitting the ball and running around the bases! What about football?

Ben: I enjoy kicking the ball and trying to score goals. It's so exciting!

Adam: Cool! Do you play football with your friends too?

Ben: Yes, we have a lot of fun matches at the park. Do you want to join us sometime?

Adam: Sure! That sounds awesome!

Interviewer: Hi there! Thanks for coming! What's your name, and why do you want to work here?

Interviewee: Hi, I'm Roeena, and I want to work at Happy Mart to make money and serve customers.

Interviewer: What do you like doing for fun?

Interviewee: I like spending time with my family and friends.

Interviewer: Teamwork is important. Tell me about a time you worked with friends or classmates.

Interviewee: We worked together to make a poster, and I led our group.

Interviewer: Nice! If a customer needs help finding something, what would you do?

Interviewee: I will ask what they're looking for and take them to that part of the store.

Interviewer: Great! Last question: What's something you're really good at?

Interviewee: I'm good at arranging things and keeping our home clean.

Interviewer: That's helpful! We'll be in touch. Thanks for coming!
Interviewee: Thank you.

QUESTIONS and ANSWERS: SELF-INTRODUCTION

1. What is your name?

My name is Geraldine Woods.

2. Where are you from?

I am from the Philippines.

3. Where do you live?

I live in Seattle.

4. How old are you?

I am 40 years old.

5. When is your birthday?

My birthday is on August 27th.

6. What is your first language?

My first language is Cebuano.

7. What do you like to do in your free time?

I enjoy reading books and watching movies.

8. What do you do?

I am a homemaker.

I work in a company.

9. Where do you work or study?

I work at home.

I study at Seattle Community College.

10. What is your favorite food?

I love pizza and chocolate ice cream.

QUESTIONS and ANSWERS: DAILY ROUTINE

1. **What time do you wake up in the morning?**
   I wake up at 4:00 am.

2. **What do you do first thing in the morning?**
   I drink tea.

3. **Did you eat breakfast?**
   Yes, I had rice and eggs for breakfast.

4. **What time do you go to school or work?**
   I go to school at 6:00 pm.
   I join the class at 6:00 pm.

5. **What is your favorite subject?**
   My favorite subject is English.

6. **Do you eat before or after class?**
   Yes, I eat before class. I usually eat a sandwich and some fruits.

7. **What do you do in the afternoon?**
   I do my homework and then take a nap.

8. **What time do you eat dinner?**
   I eat dinner at 5:30 pm.

9. **What do you like to do in the evening?**
   I read a book and watch TV.

10. **What time do you go to bed?**
    I go to bed at 10:00 pm.

QUESTIONS and ANSWERS: MY FAMILY

1. How many people are in your family?

There are four people in my family – my mom, my dad, my sister, and me.

There are five people in my family – my husband, three children, and me.

2. What are your parents' names?

My mother's name is Nida, and my father's name is Gene.

3. Do you have any siblings?

Yes, I have one sister. Her name is Gladys.

No, I don't.

4. How old is your brother/sister?

My sister is 31 years old.

5. Where do your parents and siblings live?

They live in the Philippines.

6. What do your mother and father do for work?

My mother is a homemaker, and my father is a teacher.

7. What does your husband/wife do for work?

My husband works for the government.

8. What are your children's names, and how old are they?

My daughters are Devine (18 years old), Nicole (16 years old), and Junior (5 months old).

9. Do you have any pets?

Yes, we have a dog named Max.

No, I don't.

10. What do you like to do with your family on weekends?

On weekends, we go to the park or stay at home..

QUESTIONS and ANSWERS: AT HOME

1. What is your home like?
My home is comfortable.

2. Who do you live with?
I live with my husband and children: Devine, Nicole, and Junior.

3. How many bedrooms are there in your house?
There are two bedrooms in my house.

4. What is your favorite place in your house?
My favorite place is the kitchen because I like to cook and eat.

5. What is your favorite thing in your house?
My favorite thing in my house is my bed.

6. What do you do at home?
I care for my family, clean, do laundry, wash dishes, and cook meals.

7. What do you like to do at home for fun?
I like to watch movies.
I like watching movies.

8. Do you have a garden/balcony at home?
No, I don't. / Yes, I do.
No, we don't. / Yes, we do.

9. How long have you been living in your home?
We have lived here for three years.

10. What is your complete home address?
It's 10000 10th Avenue NW, Apartment M-11 Seattle, WA 98100.

QUESTIONS and ANSWERS: AT THE DOCTOR'S CLINIC

1. What's the matter?
   I have a headache.

2. What is the problem?
   I have a fever and a sore throat.

3. When did you start feeling this way?
   It started yesterday.

4. Have you had a cough for a long time?
   No, it started two days ago.

5. Are you allergic to any medicine?
   No, I'm not allergic to any medicine.

6. Do you have any health problems?
   No, I'm healthy.

7. Are you taking any medicine now?
   Yes, I'm taking antibiotics.

8. How is the pain on a scale from 1 to 10?
   It's a 7.

9. Are you feeling like you want to throw up?
   Yes, I might throw up.

10. Do you want a medicine to make you feel better?
   Yes, please. No, thank you.

QUESTIONS and ANSWERS: AT SCHOOL

1. Where do you study?

   I study at Seattle Community College.

2. Do you study online or in person?

   I study online.

3. What time does your class start and end?

   My class starts at 6:00 pm and ends at 8:50 pm.

4. What days do you study in school?

   I study from Monday to Thursday.

5. Who is your teacher?

   My teacher is Geraldine Woods.

6. What is your favorite subject in school?

   My favorite subject is English.

7. Do you have any friends at school?

   Yes, I have friends: Joseph, Mary, Ana, and Peter.

8. What do you do during break time in class?

   I eat.

9. What do you use to study?

   I use my workbook, notebook, pencil, eraser, and laptop.

10. Why do you study English?

   I study English because I want to make many friends and find a job.

QUESTIONS and ANSWERS: CLASS

1. What do you do?

I am a student. I am a homemaker. I work for a company.

2. Where do you study/work?

I study at Seattle Community College.

I work at the mall.

I don't work.

3. What time does your class start and end?

It starts at 6 pm and ends at 8:50 pm.

4. What do you like about your class?

I like speaking, reading, writing, and listening.

I like writing, reading, and grammar.

5. How long have you been studying English?

I have been studying English in America for 6 months.

I have been studying English for 1 year.

6. Do you study with other people?

Yes, I study with other students.

7. What do you do every day in class?

Every day, I study grammar, practice speaking, reading, and writing.

8. What do you use to study?

I use my laptop, pen, workbook, notebook, and sometimes my phone.

I use television, video, Zoom, phone, notebook, and books.

9. What's your daily study schedule?

I usually study from Monday to Thursday, from 6:00 to 8:50 pm.

10. Do you have any plans or goals for your school in the future?

In the future, I want to speak English with many people.

QUESTIONS and ANSWERS: PLACES

1. Do you buy fruits and vegetables?

Yes, I buy fruits and vegetables at the grocery store.

2. Where do you buy books?

I buy books at the mall.

3. Where do you go to see a doctor when you are not feeling well?

I go to a clinic near our house.

4. Where do you buy clothes and shoes?

I buy clothes and shoes at the mall.

5. Do you study in-person at school or online?

I study online.

6. Where do you go to send letters and packages?

I go to the post office.

7. What place do you go to have a nice meal?

I go to a restaurant to have a nice meal.

I cook at home.

8. Where can you get money or cash?

I can get money from the bank.

I can get money at the ATM.

9. What place can you visit to enjoy nature and have a picnic?

I can visit the park to enjoy nature and have a picnic.

10. Where do you go to catch a bus or train?

I go to the bus station.

I go to the train station.

QUESTIONS and ANSWERS: SHOPPING

1. What do you like to buy when you go shopping?
   I like to buy clothes and food when I go shopping.

2. Where do you usually go shopping with your family?
   I go shopping with my family at Walco.

3. Do you prefer shopping online or going to a store?
   I like going to the store because I like walking around.

4. What's your favorite store?
   My favorite store is Walco!

5. Do you have a favorite piece of clothing you like to wear?
   Yes, I have a favorite black dress.

6. How do you feel when you get something new from the store?
   I feel happy and excited!

7. What's the last thing you bought?
   The last thing I bought was a pair of shoes.
   I bought shoes, pants, and shirt.

8. What would you like to buy with your own money?
   I want to buy books.

9. Have you ever lost something while shopping?
   Yes, once I lost my wallet, but I found it later.

10. Is there something you really want to buy but haven't been able to get yet?
    Yes, I really want to buy a new computer. I'm saving money.

QUESTIONS and ANSWERS: HOBBIES

1. What do you like to do for fun?
   I like drawing pictures.

2. Do you have a favorite hobby?
   Yes, my favorite hobby is listening to music.

3. What can you do for hours and not get bored?
   I can read books for hours.

4. Do you like sports?
   No, I don't like sports. I prefer playing board games.
   Yes, I do. I like football.

5. What's your favorite thing to do on weekends?
   I enjoy spending time with my family on weekends.

6. Do you have any special hobbies you do with your friends?
   Yes, we like to cook together.

7. Can you play a musical instrument?
   Yes, I can play the piano.

8. What hobby makes you happy?
   Watching movies makes me happy.

9. Do you like doing things outdoors or indoors?
   I prefer indoor activities.

10. How do you relax after a busy day?
    I relax by listening to music.

QUESTIONS and ANSWERS: MY FAVORITE FOOD

1. What is your favorite food?

My favorite food is pizza.

2. Why do you like it?

I like pizza because it's delicious and has lots of toppings.

3. How often do you eat your favorite food?

I eat pizza every week.

4. Do you prefer homemade or restaurant pizza?

I prefer restaurant pizza because it's really tasty.

5. What toppings do you like on your pizza?

I like pepperoni and mushrooms on my pizza.

6. What is your favorite dessert?

My favorite dessert is ice cream.

7. What flavor of ice cream do you like?

I like chocolate ice cream.

8. Do you enjoy cooking or baking your favorite food?

I enjoy cooking at home with my family.

9. What food do you dislike or avoid?

I don't like bitter food.

10. If you could have any food right now, what would it be?

I would love to have a crispy fried chicken right now.

REFERENCES

Diaz, B., Magy, R., & Salas-Isnardi, F. (2017). Future Intro Student Book with MyEnglishLab (Edition 1). Pearson Education.

Foley, B. H., & Neblett, E. R. (2001). Basic Grammar in Action: An Integrated Course in English (First Edition). Heinle ELT.

Gianola, A. (2000). Stories Plus: Readings and Activities. New Readers Pr.

Hartel, J. A., Lowry, B., & Hendon, W. (2005). Sam and Pat Book 1: Beginning Reading and Writing (1st Edition). Heinle ELT.

Heyer, S. (2005). All New Very Easy True Stories: A Picture-Based First Reader (First Edition). Pearson Longman.

Huizenga, J. (2004). The Heinle Picture Dictionary (Monolingual English Edition) (unknown Edition). Thomson Heinle.

Nishio, Y. (2006). Longman ESL Literacy Student Book, 3rd Edition (3rd Edition). Pearson Longman.

Rouse, J. C. (2010). Future English for Results. 2, Teacher's Edition and Lesson Planner. Pearson.